FOOD OF THE FARMLANDS, SEA, LAKES AND FORESTS

Cuisine from Sweden's West at its Best

"Cuisine from Sweden's West at its Best"
was created, designed and produced by Nordbok International ab, Box 7095, Gothenburg, Sweden

❧

Editorial staff
Karl Beijbom, Gunnar Stenmar, Anders Walberg, Gunnar Winald

❧

Coordinating team
Håkan Ridal, Project Leader, County Administration of Västra Götaland
Ann-Charlotte Dahlstedt, Project Secretary, County Administration of Västra Götaland
Linn Sandberg, Vin & Sprit AB, Stockholm
Birgitta Ullerås, Västra Götaland Rural Economy and Agricultural Society
Ulf Wagner, restaurateur, Fiskekrogen, Gothenburg
Gunvor Fröberg, University of Gothenburg
Ann Katrin Ljung, GT/Expressen, Gothenburg
Per Orgert, SHR, Sweden's Hotel & Restaurant Owners, Gothenburg

❧

Graphic design and Art director
Claes Franzén

Typography and Ad assistant
Kajsa Andersson

Photographer
Karin Mönefors

Coordinating chef
Dan Lexö
Gunilla Lexö (food styling) Karl Bengtsson (beverage suggestions)

Illustrations
Ulf Sveningson

Recipe research
Gunvor Fröberg, Britt Hallberg, Siri Reuterstrand

English recipe translation and adaptation
Melody Favish

Text translation
Jon van Leuven

Repro
Hansen Media, Gothenburg

❧

Printed by Elanders Gummesson, Falköping

World Copyright© 1999-12-03 Nordbok International

ISBN 91-7442-046-1

FOOD OF THE FARMLANDS, SEA, LAKES AND FORESTS

Cuisine from Sweden's West at its Best

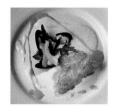

NORDBOK INTERNATIONAL AB

Contents

Desserts

Baked goods

Schnapps

West is best

Recipes in alphabetical order see page 198

Winners in the Cookbook Contest

Festive menus

FIRST PRIZE
Arne Petersen, Tidaholm RECIPES PAGES 26–29

SECOND PRIZE
Karen Pilgaard, Tibro RECIPES PAGES 30–33

THIRD PRIZE
Joakim Funk, Skövde RECIPES PAGES 34–37

Individual dishes

TIED FIRST PRIZE
Meta Bruto, Bovallstrand RECIPES PAGES 108

TIED FIRST PRIZE
Annika Dalbert, Åsnebyn RECIPES PAGES 100

SECOND PRIZE
Lars Gillis Larsson, Gothenburg RECIPES PAGES 134

THIRD PRIZE
Gunilla Wahrnberg, Ed RECIPES PAGES 102

Schnapps

FIRST PRIZE
Ulf Larsson and A M Alströmer, Alingsås RECIPES PAGES 179

SECOND PRIZE
Bo Karlsson, Karlskoga RECIPES PAGES 177

THIRD PRIZE
Lennart Granqvist, Tidaholm RECIPES PAGES 180

Members of the food jury
GÖTE BERNHARDSSON, COUNTY GOVERNOR, CHAIRMAN, ULF WAGNER, FISKEKROGEN, GOTHENBURG,
SOLVEIG BJÖRCKE, UNIVERSITY OF GOTHENBURG, GOTHENBURG, STEFAN GRYNGE, LYON RESTAURANT SCHOOL, SKÖVDE,
ANN KATRIN LJUNG, GT/EXPRESSEN, GOTHENBURG, MAGARETA FROST JOHANSSON, VÄSTRA GÖTALAND RURAL ECONOMY AND AGRICULTURAL SOCIETY

Members of the schnapps jury
GÖTE BERNHARDSSON, CHAIRMAN, LINN SANDBERG, CURT DAHLSTRÖM AND FOLKE ANDERSSON, VIN & SPRIT AB, RICKARD HALLERÖD, RONNUM MANOR

We congratulate the winners and thank everyone who participated in the competition.

7

CUISINE FROM SWEDEN'S WEST AT ITS BEST

Cuisine from Sweden's West at its Best – a delicious success!

Great enthusiasm has greeted this book and, without doubt, also the "Food of the Farm-lands, Sea, Lakes and Forests" in "Festive Menus and Family Recipes" that it contains. You are now holding the fourth edition of *Cuisine from Sweden's West at its Best*.

We have printed more than 50,000 copies and published the book in Swedish, English, German and French. Appreciated everywhere and in many languages, it presents sumptuous and tasty food prepared with recipes submitted from all over the county.

The concept behind *Cuisine from Sweden's West at its Best* is to display Västra Götaland as a "food county". This is the largest food-producing region in Sweden. The western Swedish food industry has considerable importance and employs more than 25,000 people.

Our raw materials come from coastal waters and inland lakes, from the forests and the farms that dot our landscape. This has inspired one author in the book to rhyme:

"Västra Götaland is the world's best pantry. We who live there heartily agree!"

In order to illuminate the subject, I decided to sponsor a recipe contest featuring the food and drink of western Sweden and to collect all the winning recipes in a book. The results were approximately 150 recipes for appetizers, main dishes, desserts, and festive menus, along with appropriate beverage suggestions ranging from water to wine, beer to schnapps. And there are more than 300 colorful photographs of the winning entries and views of the county.

Seeing the results of the contest become a book has been an exciting journey. Most of these recipes were entries in the contest, which attracted inhabitants from all over our county. Some recipes were developed by outstanding local chefs.

This book also includes interesting observations on the history and culture of western Sweden, as well as entertaining anecdotes about the joys of eating, by prominent county residents.

I know that *Cuisine from Sweden's West at its Best* has contributed to many good meals in the company of family and friends. Moreover, I know that it has provided "armchair chefs" with hours of delectable reading.

Through such popularity it has not only earned a well-deserved place in western Swedish homes, but also spread the word of our county's cuisine to guests and tourists from near and far. Numerous municipalities, companies and authorities have used the book as a perfect representative gift.

So here we are at the fourth edition! It confirms that the vision of a food county is valid, that the book has gladdened thousands of people and, in short, that this has been a venture of lasting quality.

Once again, dear friends of good food: may you enjoy delicious meals and pleasant reading!

Göteborg, June 2005

Göte Bernhardsson
Governor of the County of Västra Götaland

HAVET, INSJÖARNA, JORDEN, SKOGEN

VÄSTRA GÖTALAND ÄR VÄRLDENS BÄSTA SKAFFERI
TACK FÖR ATT VI FÅR BO DÄRI ♥♥♥♥

All this is your land, all this is my land
From the shrimp of Smögen to Vättern's whitefish
From Hönö's flatbread to Gullspång's salmon
Västra Götaland is made for you and me

From earth and forests, from seas and islands
To old wood tables and new white napkins
In huts and castles, from daily bread to famous feasting
Our county is made for you and me

Anders Westgårdh

(AFTER A SONG BY WOODY GUTHRIE)

A county resident praises its pantry

HONORED GUESTS! I am not a public speaker, but on behalf of the 1,500,000 residents of the county, I would like to express our gratitude for all the wonderful food we have here.

I am both eternally grateful and deeply thankful that we in Västra Götaland have the privilege of living in the world's geographical equivalent of a balanced diet chart. Almost everything desirable in the way of food is available within our borders – from herring to dill, from pork to soft drinks – there's not much missing here. A person could live an entire lifetime here without tiring of the great gastronomic buffet produced right here in our own county.

Consider the potato, which is practically a western Swedish invention. Our thanks to you, Jonas Alströmer. Your homely tuber is the basis of our diet, and we cannot fathom a life without potatoes. Just imagine, a hamburger and soft drink with fried turnip sticks, or even worse, herring and schnapps… with rice?

In Alingsås, the potato's home country, there is a huge festival every year in its honor. In Rio de Janeiro, hardly anybody knows why the carnival takes place, but here, we are conscious of our origins and our culinary roots. Another example is Whitefish Day in Hjo. Such a rapturous attitude regarding the interplay between spirit and matter would be difficult to duplicate. In addition, I want to thank all those devoted souls in the county, who, year after year, arrange culinary events for public enjoyment. Shrimp Day in Strömstad also deserves mention.

Now, I would like to tell you about when I became aware of the richness of our local culinary landscape. It has to do with shrimp. The year may have been 1992, and for some reason, we were spending the night in a pretty little wooden boat moored at the ferry berth on Hamburg island. We were a

group of 16 year old boys, and we hadn't given much thought to food. We had plenty of beer, and maybe a can of baked beans. But by evening, after the sun had set, our stomachs began to growl. They needed more than malt and hops. As if our hunger were visible on his depth-sounder, an old fisherman came toward us. He slowed down at the pier where we sat and shouted, "Would you like some shrimp, boys?" Without waiting for an answer, he handed over a big bag brimming with the sort of powerful, meaty, roe-filled, wonderful shrimp that exist only in the waters between Smögen and Fjällbacka. Nowhere else, at least not just then.

We ate greedily and in silence. It was a defining moment in my life. For that reason, I thank all you old fishermen.

That shrimp orgy took place a long time ago, and many more interesting tidbits have gone through my digestive system since then, including crocodile. Over the years, I have been lucky enough to travel in distant lands and brave enough to try just about any local specialty. I have eaten swordfish in the Caribbean, dined at a United Nations gala in New York, enjoyed oysters at Place Madeleine in Brussels and fresh octopus on Greek islands smaller than a city block.

And yet, when all is said and done, it is not Champagne in France or cajun stew in Louisiana that I consider the culinary high

points in my life. Rather, the shrimp in Hamburgsund, the trout in Lake Vättern, the roast moose at Bullis in Lidköping, and Inga's homemade bread on Dyr island. It's the mackerel which I caught with my grandfather at Moose island, and the Easter salmon that Janne brought home from Vänern, and - last but not least – my dear wife's ocean crayfish gratin. The best I have eaten has been on home turf.

Our kitchens are full of machines and equipment for making food preparation easier. There is a chrome Italian gadget for making fresh pasta, and the ice cream maker has given us many delicious desserts. The food processor takes the toil out of chopping, and toast literally pops out of the toaster every morning. Still, I would happily give them all away, except for one thing: The egg-cheese mold. Egg-cheese is so good that the very thought brings tears to my eyes as I write these words. In this context, thanks to Osvald for the beautiful hand-carved mold, and thanks to Grandmother Karin for the handwritten recipe which is the difference between success and fiasco at family dinners and parties. Speaking of egg-cheese, it is often served at the fantastic restaurant at Bohuslän's museum in

Uddevalla. You should make a pilgrimage there some time, all of you.

And as long as we are on the subject of cheese, you also should visit the dairy at Falbygden next time you drive to Falköping. It is a wonderful temple of gastronomy where the culinary greatness of the entire county is concentrated in a small wedge of aged cheese, which makes your palate quiver with delight. So hearty thanks to all cheese farmers and dairy workers.

In this same context, we should not forget all the hard-working chefs and restaurateurs who, over the past 10 years, have made Gothenburg the nation's gastronomic capital. This is true. In relation to its size, Gothenburg has more good restaurants than Stockholm, Copenhagen and Oslo. And we won't even mention Helsinki.

The best ingredients prepared with care and creativity of the highest caliber have become Gothenburg's trademark. I'd like to thank all the visionaries, from the pioneer, Leif Mannerström to the young master, Karl Ljung.

Yes, my friends, we live in a wonderful part of the world. If we have anything to complain about, it would have to be the climate. It would be wonderful if we could grow olives, or if asparagus could be picked already in May and as fat as those in Alsace.

But we can't have everything. And really, all I miss is wine.

On the other hand, we are reading a lot about global warming. Maybe in a hundred years, there will be Riesling grapes growing along the banks of the Göta River. Let's raise our glasses to that right now!

In conclusion:

Get a piece of parchment paper and trace the contours of the County of Västra Götaland. Then move it around on a map of the world. How long does it take to find another area equally small with such a bounty of food?

A good while, I imagine. Our wealth of foodstuffs in such a tiny area has to be close to unique.

Granted, there are probably areas of France and Italy which are veritable bread-baskets. And New England in the US has lobsters and cows which are practically the same size. The southeastern part of Australia is another rich larder.

But do they have hönö flatbread with liver paté and pickles? No, they don't. So, to simplify matters with a local patriot's proud touch of exaggeration, I can state the following:

Västra Götaland is probably the world's best pantry.

We who live there heartily agree.

Anders Westgårdh

Festive Menus

LEIF MANNERSTRÖM has had an enormous influence on Swedish gastronomy. He has inspired many young chefs to reach for the top. Today, his flagship is Sjömagasinet, which has earned a well-deserved star in Guide Michelin. And when the master himself is working in the kitchen, everything is just so good!

Crab and turbot are among the best our western shores can offer. Mannerström's appetizer has a rich shellfish flavor, and the fish a robust salty character. Both are served with classic side dishes.

All recipes serve four.

Appetizer
CRAB AND ANCHOVY STARTER

Main dish
SALT-BAKED TURBOT

Dessert
WHITE CHOCOLATE CHEESECAKE

Crab and anchovy starter

2 female crabs, cooked
8 Swedish-style anchovy fillets
3-4 tablespoons chopped fresh chives
3-4 tablespoons chopped fresh dill
2 tablespoons mayonnaise
salt and pepper
4 slices toasted white bread
mixed greens
mustard sauce (see page 190)

Remove crabmeat from shells and cut into small pieces. Coarsely chop anchovies. Combine crabmeat, anchovies, chives, dill and mayonnaise. Season with salt and pepper. Spoon mixture onto toast. Garnish with greens. Drizzle a little mustard sauce all around.

BEVERAGE SUGGESTION: Mustard sauce makes wine selection a problem. But it's difficult to say no to a glass of champagne or other dry sparkling wine with this lovely starter.

NAVEN LIGHTHOUSE

Salt-baked turbot

1 whole turbot,
about 2 1/2 - 3 kg
(5-6 lb)
1 kg (2 1/4 lb)
coarse salt
600 g (1 1/3 lb)
potatoes
100 g (3 1/2 oz)
unsalted butter
2 hard-cooked
eggs
3-4 tablespoons
chopped chives
salt and pepper
2 tablespoons
grated fresh
horseradish

Preheat oven to 150°C (300°F). Rinse turbot thoroughly, then dry well. Sprinkle a 1 cm (1/2") layer of coarse salt in an oven pan. Place fish on the salt, then cover completely with remaining salt. Bake about 40 minutes, until it reaches an internal temperature of 58°C (137°F) at its thickest part. Peel and boil potatoes. Melt butter and chop eggs. Slice potatoes and combine with butter, eggs and chives. Season with salt, pepper and horseradish. Serve alongside fish.

SERVING SUGGESTION:
A mustard hollandaise sauce goes well with this dish.

BEVERAGE SUGGESTION: Turbot, simply prepared, but what a wonderful flavor it has – it's king of the sea. And it should be served with the king of white wines – a Chablis! Preferably a Chablis Grand Cru, if budget allows.

White chocolate cheesecake

2 dl (3/4 cup)
digestive biscuit
or graham cracker
crumbs
25 g (2 table-
spoons) melted
butter
60 g (2 oz) white
chocolate
50 g (1/4 cup)
sugar
400 g (14 oz)
cream cheese,
softened
2 eggs

Preheat oven to 175°C (350°F). Combine biscuit crumbs and butter. Press into (4") four 10 cm tartlet tins or one 20 cm (8") springform pan. Bake about 10 minutes. Reduce temperature to 140°C (275°F). Melt chocolate in a water bath. Beat sugar and cream cheese until light and fluffy. Add eggs, one at a time, beating well after each. Mix melted chocolate into a small amount of the cheese mixture. Then add to remaining cheese mixture, beating until thoroughly combined. Pour over pre-baked crust. Bake individual tartlets 12-13 minutes, springform about 40 minutes, until edges are just set. Serve at room temperature, garnished with berries.

BEVERAGE SUGGESTION: Chocolate is difficult to pair with wine. White chocolate is somewhat easier, especially when it is tempered with cream cheese and eggs. A rather full-bodied sweet white wine, preferably from Australia, is a good choice.

ULF WAGNER
FISKEKROGEN, GÖTEBORG

Ulf Wagner's restaurant, *The Place*, was the first in western Sweden to be awarded a star in Guide Michelin. Today, his talents can be enjoyed at Fiskekrogen. Ulf is known for his culinary creativity, with flavorful combinations and an absolute insistence upon the very best ingredients.

His cod-herring appetizer may become a new smörgåsbord classic. The next course is free-range chicken from Bo Mowitz in Trollhättan. At a time when most Swedes had to endure factory-farmed birds, Mowitz concentrated on raising birds as flavorful as the famous Bresse chickens of France.

All recipes serve six.

Appetizer
CHEF NORDSTRÖM'S
"COD-HERRING"

Main dish
SCALLOP-STUFFED BREAST OF FREE-RANGE
CHICKEN WITH VEGETABLE GRATIN,
CRISPY MUSHROOM ROLL
AND CIDER-CHIVE BEURRE BLANC

Dessert
CRÈME BRÛLÉE WITH BLACKBERRY COMPOTE

Chef Nordström's "cod-herring"

1 kg (2 1/4 lb) center-cut cod from a 5-6 kg (10-12 lb) fish
fleur de sel – French gourmet salt
brine from Swedish-style anchovies

Horseradish sauce:
1 1/2 dl (2/3 cup) sour cream
1/2 dl (3 1/2 tablespoons) mayonnaise
4 tablespoons (1/4 cup) grated horseradish
1/2 teaspoon sugar
1 teaspoon lemon juice
salt and pepper

Mustard sauce:
1 1/2 dl (2/3 cup) mustard sauce (see page 190)
1/2 dl (3 1/2 tablespoons) crème fraiche
or dairy sour cream
1 tablespoon sweet mustard
1 tablespoon Dijon-style mustard
2 tablespoons chopped dill

Red wine and onion sauce:
1 dl (1/2 cup) red wine
1/2 dl (1/4 cup) water
1 dl (1/2 cup) sugar
1/2 dl (1/4 cup) vinegar
1 small red onion, sliced
1 bay leaf
5 allspice berries
5 white peppercorns

Rub cod with salt and several tablespoons anchovy brine. Marinate 5-6 hours in a cool place. Preheat oven to 100°C (210°F). Bake cod about 20-25 minutes, until it reaches an internal temperature of 55°C (130°F) at its thickest part. The cod should not be completely cooked, as it finishes cooking in the marinades. Refrigerate. "Pluck" cod into slices.

HORSERADISH SAUCE:
Combine all ingredients and add one-third of the cod.

MUSTARD SAUCE:
Combine all ingredients and add one-third of the cod.

RED WINE AND ONION SAUCE
Combine all ingredients in a saucepan and bring to a boil. Cool, then add remaining cod.

Serve these cod-herring dishes in small dishes with crispbread, aged cheese and butter.

BEVERAGE SUGGESTION: When cod is marinated like herring, there is only one drink that works – a light beer! And a little schnapps on the side, if desired. Try flavoring schnapps with angelica – an old western Swedish tradition.

Scallop-stuffed breast of free-range chicken with vegetable gratin, crispy mushroom roll and cider-chive beurre blanc

Chicken roulade:
1 kg (2 1/4 lb) skinless and boneless
breast of free-range chicken
salt and freshly ground black pepper
8 large spinach leaves
10 medium scallops

Vegetable gratin:
1/4 eggplant
1/2 zucchini
1 1/2 red bell pepper
1 baking potato
1/2 leek
3 tomatoes
1 garlic clove

Crispy mushroom packets:
10 mushrooms
15 oyster mushrooms
2 dl (1 cup) whipping cream
1/2 dl (1/4 cup) freshly grated
parmesan cheese
6 sheets filo pastry

Cider-chive beurre blanc:
3/4 dl (1/3 cup) sugar
1 dl (scant 1/2 cup) lemon juice
5 dl (2 cups) apple cider
5 dl (2 cups) chicken stock
1 dl (scant 1/2 cup) minced shallots
salt and pepper
100 g (3 1/2 oz) unsalted butter

CHICKEN ROULADE:
Split chicken breasts lengthwise, almost completely through. Open and pound lightly. Arrange breasts, overlapping slightly, on a sheet of lightly greased aluminum foil. Season with salt and pepper. Arrange spinach over chicken. Place scallops in a long cylinder on the spinach. Roll up, enclosing spinach and scallops in the chicken. Wrap roll in foil, as tightly as possible, then seal. Preheat oven to 125°C (250°F). Bake 35-45 minutes, until it reaches an internal temperature of 63°C (145°F). Remove and let rest at least 10 minutes. Slice.

VEGETABLE GRATIN:
Preheat oven to 150°C (300°F). Thinly slice all vegetables lengthwise. Sauté potato slices in butter. Add garlic and sauté 5 more minutes. Layer with remaining vegetables in an ovenproof dish. Bake about 20 minutes, until tender. Remove and cool under pressure.

CRISPY MUSHROOM ROLLS:
Slice mushrooms and brown in a dry non-stick pan. Reduce cream over high heat until half the original amount remains. Pour cream over mushrooms, then fold in cheese. Season with salt and pepper. Chill. Preheat oven to 175°C (350°F). Place 1/6 of the mushroom mixture on each filo sheet, then fold over the edges and roll up.

CIDER-CHIVE BEURRE BLANC:
Heat sugar in a dry saucepan until melted and golden brown. Add lemon juice, cider, chicken stock and shallots. Reduce over high heat until one-third of the original amount remains. Strain, then whisk in butter in pats. Do not allow to boil after butter is added.

BEVERAGE SUGGESTION: This is a complex dish with many flavors, and the cider adds a fruity character. It needs a fruity and complex white wine. Good choices are either a Riesling from Australia or a dry Muscat from the south of France.

Crème brûlée with blackberry compote

Brûlée mixture:
1 1/2 dl (2/3 cup) full
fat milk
2 1/2 dl (1 cup)
whipping cream
1 vanilla bean, split
1/2 teaspoon ground
cardamom
3 egg yolks
60 g (1/3 cup) sugar
brown sugar

Blackberry compote:
1/2 dl (3 1/2 tablespoons)
sugar
200 g (7-8 oz) frozen
blackberries
1/2 tablespoon cornstarch

CRÈME BRÛLÉE:
Preheat oven to 100°C (210°F). Scald milk, cream, vanilla bean and cardamom. Beat egg yolks and sugar until light and lemon-colored. Remove vanilla bean, then gradually add milk mixture. Pour into six individual custard cups and bake until just set, about 30 minutes. Preheat grill. Sprinkle custards with brown sugar and grill until sugar has melted and turned brown.
Stir sugar into berries and defrost slowly. Strain off the juices, whisk in cornstarch and bring to a boil. Simmer until thickened. Cool, then fold in berries.

BEVERAGE SUGGESTION: :
Crème brûlée is a classic dessert, and served with berry compote, it works with most sweet white wines. Sauternes or a Tokay 5 puttonyos are two classic choices.

SCALLOP-STUFFED BREAST OF FREE-RANGE CHICKEN WITH VEGETABLE GRATIN,
CRISPY MUSHROOM ROLL AND CIDER-CHIVE BEURRE BLANC

DAN LEXÖ
LASSE-MAJAS KROG, MARSTRAND

Enjoying a meal created by Dan Lexö is a pleasurable experience, from the first line on the menu to the last morsel of food. This master chef unites his joy of food and good humor with extensive professional skill. Here he presents a festive menu with schnapps, starting with a beautiful shellfish appetizer, followed by flounder with vermouth sauce and a luxurious pudding and pancake dessert.

This pancake is a time-honored tradition in the cherry-growing area around Skaraborg. "We used to see who could spit the pits the farthest," says Dan. In the summer, Dan runs *Lasse-Majas Krog* on Marstrand. During the winter, he is a very busy consultant.

All recipes serve four.

Appetizer
SEAFOOD SALAD
BEVERAGE: A TALL BEER AND
A COLD OP ANDERSSON

❧

Main dish
CRISPY FRIED FLOUNDER WITH
CREAMY MUSSELS, FENNEL AND CARROTS
SERVED WITH VERMOUTH SAUCE
BEVERAGE: LÄCKÖ CASTLE AQUAVIT

❧

Dessert
CREAM PUDDING WITH PANCAKES
AND CHERRY SAUCE
BEVERAGE: BLACK CURRANT SCHNAPPS

Seafood salad

1/2 dl (3 1/2 tablespoons) mayonnaise
2 dl (3 1/4 cup) crème fraîche
or dairy sour cream
12 cooked ocean crayfish tails,
chopped if large
200 g (7 oz) cooked shelled shrimp
3-4 tablespoons chopped chives
or scallions
3-4 tablespoons chopped dill
50 g (1/2 cup) sliced mushrooms
80 g (3/4 cup) shredded snow peas
2 tablespoons grated horseradish
salt and freshly ground white pepper

Dill oil:
1 dl (1/3 cup) chopped dill
1 dl (1/3 cup) olive oil

spiced tea cake (see page 166)
or plain focaccia, cut into wedges
100 g (4 oz) arugula
4 tablespoons lumpfish caviar
dill fronds
lemon wedges

Combine mayonnaise and crème fraiche. Fold in remaining ingredients. Season with salt and pepper.
Puree dill and oil in a food processor until smooth.
Place a wedge of teacake on each plate. Top with arugula and seafood salad. Top with a spoonful of caviar. Garnish with dill and lemon. Drizzle dill oil all around.

BEVERAGE SUGGESTION:
A tall beer and a cold
OP Andersson.

Crispy fried flounder with creamy mussels, fennel and carrots, served with vermouth sauce

Mussels:
about 30 fresh mussels
1 fennel bulb
1 tablespoon olive oil
1 shallot, minced
2 garlic cloves, minced
1 carrot, in batons
3 dl (1 1/4 dl) white wine

Vermouth sauce:
1 shallot, minced
fennel trimmings
1 tablespoon olive oil
5 dl (2 cups) rich fish stock
mussel stock (from cooking the mussels)
3 dl (1 1/4 cups) whipping cream
1/2 dl (3 1/2 tablespoons) dry vermouth
2 teaspoons cornstarch
1/8 teaspoon cayenne pepper
lemon juice
salt and white pepper

Flounder:
4 double fillets of flounder
1 dl (1/3cup) flour
1 egg yolk beaten with
1 tablespoon water
2 dl (1 cup) breadcrumbs
2 tablespoons butter
salt and freshly ground
white pepper
chopped parsley

Scrub mussels well. Cut fennel into batons. Chop remaining fennel and reserve for sauce. Heat olive oil in a saucepan, add mussels and vegetables and sauté a couple of minutes. Add wine, cover and simmer about 5 minutes, until mussels have opened. Discard mussels which have not opened. Strain, reserving stock for sauce. Chill. Remove meat from shells, saving a few shells for garnish. Puree 5-6 mussels with 2 dl (3/4 cup) vermouth sauce. Strain. Reheat mussel sauce, mussels, carrot and fennel. Season with salt and freshly ground white pepper.

VERMOUTH SAUCE:
Sauté onion and fennel in olive oil. Add fish and mussel stock and simmer until about 2 dl (3/4 cup) remains. Add cream and vermouth and simmer about 5 minutes. Thicken with cornstarch stirred into 1 tablespoon water. Season with cayenne pepper, lemon juice, salt and pepper.

FLOUNDER:
Fold fillets head to tail. Dip first in flour, then in egg, and finally in breadcrumbs. Fry in butter until golden brown, about 5 minutes per side. Season with salt and pepper. Arrange a few shells on each plate. Top with mussels and place the fish alongside. Spoon vermouth sauce all around. Drizzle a little mussel sauce around the fish. Garnish with parsley and serve with new potatoes, if available.

BEVERAGE SUGGESTION: Läckö Castle aquavit

Cream pudding with pancakes and cherry sauce

Cream pudding:
5 dl (2 cups)
whipping cream
1/2 dl (3 1/2 tablespoons)
sugar
50 g (2 oz) finely chopped
fresh ginger
2 gelatin sheets

Cherry sauce:
200 g (7-8 oz) cherries
5 dl (2 1/4 cups) red wine
1 dl (1/2 cup) Madeira
1 dl (1/2 cup) sugar
1 vanilla bean, split
1 tablespoon cornstarch
sugar

Pancakes:
4 large eggs
1 teaspoon salt
1/2 dl (3 1/2 tablespoons)
corn oil
3 dl (1 1/4 cups) flour
6 dl (2 1/2 cups)
full fat milk
butter
confectioner's sugar

CREAM PUDDING:
In a saucepan, bring cream, sugar and ginger to a boil. Simmer over low heat about 30 minutes. Then bring to a boil once more. Soak gelatin sheets in cold water to soften, about 10 minutes. Squeeze excess water from gelatin sheets and melt in hot cream mixture. Pour into four individual molds and refrigerate until set. To serve, dip in hot water about 20 seconds, then unmold.

CHERRY SAUCE:
Rinse cherries and remove stems. Bring wine, Madeira, sugar and vanilla to a boil. Lower heat and simmer about 30 minutes. Return to a boil, then add cherries. Simmer slowly about 10 minutes. Remove cherries with a slotted spoon and reserve. Remove vanilla bean and discard. Reduce cooking liquid until two-thirds of the original amount remains. Thicken with cornstarch stirred into 1 tablespoon cold water. Return cherries to sauce. Sprinkle with sugar to prevent a skin from forming. Refrigerate.

PANCAKES:
Combine eggs, salt and oil in a bowl. Whisk in flour, then milk. Let batter rest at least one hour. Heat griddle, melt butter, then make small pancakes. Unmold puddings near the center of individual serving plates. Place two pancakes alongside and sprinkle with confectioner's sugar. Arrange cherries alongside and drizzle sauce all around.

BEVERAGE SUGGESTION: Black currant schnapps

CRISPY FRIED FLOUNDER WITH CREAMY MUSSELS, FENNEL AND CARROTS,
SERVED WITH VERMOUTH SAUCE

ARNE PETERSEN
AMU GRUPPEN SKÖVDE

G RILLED TROUT FROM Vättern, an exquisite filet of roe deer and a beautiful ice cream dessert – the jury loved that menu.
Vättern trout is one of the finest freshwater fish in Sweden. According to first-prize winner, Arne Petersen, it can compete with any saltwater fish. He wraps his roe deer filet in leek and crepinette, which holds the meat in shape and seals in all the good flavors. Arne works as an educational consultant for restaurants and institutional kitchens. He has always been interested in food, perhaps because his father was a pastry chef and the aroma of newly baked bread often permeated the kitchen in his home.

All recipes serve four.

Appetizer
SAUTÉED TROUT ON A BED OF
CITRUS-MARINATED ROOT VEGETABLES
WITH SWEETENED DILL OIL

Main dish
FILET OF ROE DEER IN CREPINETTE,
WITH POTATO-CHEESE PIE,
RED ONION MARMALADE AND PORT WINE JUS

Dessert
VANILLA ICE CREAM IN A CRISPY CARAMEL BASKET
WITH APPLE CHIPS AND
LIGHTLY SWEETENED BLUEBERRY SAUCE

Sautéed trout on a bed of citrus-marinated root vegetables with sweetened dill oil

3 medium carrots
1 medium black salsify
juice of 1 lemon
1 tablespoon chopped dill
salt and pepper
1/2 teaspoon raw sugar
1/2 - 1 dl (1/3 cup) olive oil
4 trout fillets, skin on,
about 280 g (10 oz)
butter

Shred carrots and black salsify. Sprinkle with lemon juice. Marinate four hours. Puree dill, salt, pepper and raw sugar in the food processor.
Sauté trout, skin side down, in butter. Lightly brown root vegetables in olive oil.
Arrange mounds of root vegetables on individual plates. Top with fish and drizzle with dill oil.

BEVERAGE SUGGESTION:
A full-bodied white wine goes well with trout. Especially good with this dish is a wine from the Rhône valley or the south of France made from the flavorful Marsanne grape, or a Gavi from Piedmont in northern Italy.

Filet of roe deer in crepinette, with potato-cheese pie, red onion marmalade and port wine jus

Red onion marmalade:
3 red onions
butter
1 1/2 dl (2/3 cup) dark corn syrup
1-2 tablespoons red wine vinegar

Pie:
110 g (3/4cup) flour
70 g (2 1/2 oz) margarine
2 tablespoons water
4 medium boiled potatoes, shredded
2 eggs
2 dl (3/4 cup) milk
chopped fresh thyme
salt and pepper
about 1 dl (1/2 cup) grated Swiss cheese

600 g (1 1/3 lb) roe deer filet
butter
salt and pepper
1 medium leek
crepinette (order from your butcher)

Sauce:
3 dl (1 1/4 cups) game stock
1 dl (1/2 cup) port wine
2 tablespoons red currant jelly
salt and pepper
50 g (3 tablespoons) unsalted butter

Shred red onion and sauté lightly in a little butter. Add syrup and vinegar. Simmer 35-40 minutes. Taste to make sure that sweet and sour are in balance.

For the pie, cut flour into margarine until the texture of coarse crumbs. Add water and stir until mixture forms a dough. Flatten and refrigerate one hour. Preheat oven to 225°C (425°F). Press into the bottom of a quiche pan, prick all over with a fork and bake 10-15 minutes. Cool slightly. Reduce temperature to 190°C (375°F). Arrange shredded potatoes in the pie shell.

Whisk together egg, milk and seasonings. Pour over potatoes. Top with grated cheese. Bake 20-30 minutes, until filling has set. Brown meat in butter. Season with salt and pepper. Halve leek lengthwise and rinse. Simmer in boiling salted water until crisptender. Preheat oven to 125°C (250°F). Wrap filet in leek, then wrap tightly in crepinette. Roast 15-20 minutes, until meat reaches an internal temperature of 57-62°C (138-43°F). Let rest until ready to serve.

Reduce stock over high heat until half the original amount remains. Add port wine and jelly. Simmer 10 minutes. Season with salt and pepper. Just before serving, whisk in butter. Do not allow sauce to boil after butter is added.

BEVERAGE SUGGESTION: A flavorful red wine, full or medium-bodied with moderate tannin, is good with the mild, yet distinctly gamy flavor of the roe deer. This can be a red Burgundy, a red wine from Penedés in northern Spain or a Merlot from California.

Vanilla ice cream in a caramel basket with apple chips and lightly sweetened blueberry sauce

Vanilla ice cream:
4 egg yolks
100 g (1/2 cup) sugar
5 dl (2 cups) coffee cream or half and half
1 vanilla bean, split

Caramel basket:
1 egg
1 1/2 dl (2/3 cup) sugar
1/2 dl (3 1/2 tablespoons) rolled oats
1/2 dl (3 1/2 tablespoons) hot melted butter
1 tablespoon flour
1 teaspoon baking powder

Blueberry sauce:
2 dl (1 cup) fresh or frozen blueberries
1 dl (1/2 cup) sugar
1 teaspoon confectioner's sugar

Apple chips:
2 apples
confectioner's sugar

Beat egg yolks and sugar until light and lemon-colored. Scald cream with vanilla bean. Whisk hot cream into eggs. Simmer until thickened, but do not allow to boil. Whisk until cool. Remove vanilla bean, then freeze in an ice cream machine.

Preheat oven to 200°C (400°F). Beat egg and sugar until light and lemon-colored. Stir oats into hot butter, then stir into egg mixture. Spoon mixture into four mounds on a greased cookie sheet. Bake until bubbly and almost set (they will set as they cool), 6-8 minutes. While still hot, shape into baskets over drinking glasses.

Simmer blueberries and sugar about 5 minutes. Puree in a food processor. Stir in confectioner's sugar.

Preheat oven to 120°C (250°F). Peel and core apples. Slice thinly. Arrange on a cookie sheet lined with baking parchment. Sift over confectioner's sugar and bake about 50 minutes. Cool on the sheet.

To serve, place baskets on individual plates. Place a scoop of ice cream in each. Top with apple chips. Spoon sauce all around.

BEVERAGE SUGGESTION: Rich ice cream and fresh berries marry well with a glass of cold sweet sparkling Asti Spumante from northern Italy.

FILET OF ROE DEER IN CREPINETTE, WITH POTATO-CHEESE PIE,
RED ONION MARMALADE AND PORT WINE JUS

KAREN PILGAARD
RESTAURANG ALEXANDRA, TIBRO

SECOND-PRIZE WINNER Karen Pilgaard presents a dinner for chilly winter days. She loves to pick mushrooms in the woods. "With luck, I can find funnel chanterelles into the middle of December," she says.

For the main dish, she has selected ham with honey, apple and horseradish, a fine combination of typical Swedish ingredients. And there's barley in the dessert. How did she arrive at that combination? Indeed, she learned to love barley porridge at home on the family farm in Denmark. She prepares a variation on rice à la Malta and the results are delicious.

All recipes serve four.

Appetizer

FUNNEL CHANTERELLE SOUP
WITH CHEESE CROUTONS

Main dish

HONEY-GRILLED, LIGHTLY SALTED HAM
WITH WARM APPLE SALAD AND
POTATO GRATIN WITH HORSERADISH

Dessert

BARLEY DESSERT
WITH PRESERVED CHERRIES

Funnel chanterelle soup with cheese croutons

1 1/2 liters (6 cups) funnel chanterelles or other wild mushrooms
1 tablespoon butter
1 small onion, minced
1 tablespoon flour
6 dl (2 1/2 cups) mushroom stock
salt and freshly ground black pepper
1/4 teaspoon thyme
1 teaspoon black currant jelly
2 dl (3/4 cup) whipping cream
1 tablespoon chopped parsley

Cheese croutons:
65 g (2/3 cup) flour
65 g (2/3 cup) grated Gruyere or Swiss cheese
40 g (2 1/2 tablespoons) butter
1 egg
coarse salt

Use fresh mushrooms or comparable amount of dried, soaked or frozen. Clean mushrooms and sauté in butter until all liquid is released and mushrooms start to sizzle. That brings out their nutty flavor. Add onion and sprinkle with flour. Add stock, seasonings and jelly. Simmer 8-10 minutes. Add cream and more salt, if necessary. Stir in parsley.

CHEESE CROUTONS:
Preheat oven to 200°C (400°F).
Cut flour and cheese into cold butter.
Add egg and knead into a dough.
Roll thinly and sprinkle with coarse salt.
Cut into 1 1/2 cm (3/4") cubes.
Bake 5-6 minutes. Serve alongside soup, so that each person can add to the soup as desired.

BEVERAGE SUGGESTION: In recent years, funnel chanterelles have become one of Sweden's favorite mushrooms. Serve the soup with another Swedish favorite, medium-dry Madeira.

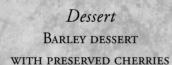

Honey-grilled, lightly salted ham with warm apple salad and potato gratin with horseradish

Ham:
1 kg (2 1/4 lb) lightly
salted ham
water
1 carrot, in chunks
1 onion, in wedges
50 g (2 oz) celeriac, sliced
2 bay leaves
5-6 allspice berries
2 tablespoons honey

Potato gratin:
1 onion
1 tablespoon grated
horseradish
1 teaspoon salt
2 1/2 dl (1 cup) light cream
1 tablespoon breadcrumbs

Apple salad:
2 sour apples
100 g (3 1/2 ounces) celeriac
10 cm (4") leek
1 tablespoon butter
1/4 teaspoon thyme
1 teaspoon vinegar

Rinse ham in cold water and place in a deep saucepan just large enough. Add water to just cover, then add vegetables and seasonings. Simmer about 1 hour, until ham reaches an internal temperature of 70°C (158°F) in its thickest part. Remove from cooking liquid and cool slightly. Just before serving, preheat oven to 200°C (400°F). Brush ham with honey and grill until honey has melted and glazed the ham.
Preheat oven to 200°C (400°F). Shred potatoes. Chop onion. Layer in a greased ovenproof dish. Whisk together horseradish, salt and cream and pour over potatoes. Sprinkle with breadcrumbs and bake about 45 minutes.
Peel and cube apples. Clean celeriac and leek. Cut celeriac into fine dice. Shred leek. Sauté apples and vegetables in butter, and season with thyme and vinegar.
To serve, divide apple salad among four individual plates. Slice ham and arrange with the salad. Garnish with fresh herbs. Serve potato gratin alongside.

BEVERAGE SUGGESTION: A fruity white wine with a little sweetness goes well with this slightly salty dish with its sweet and sour apple salad. A semi-dry German wine, preferably a Riesling, is best.

Barley dessert with preserved cherries

5 dl (2 cups) full fat milk
pinch salt
65 g (1/3 cup) pearl barley
25 g (1 oz) hazelnuts
2 tablespoons sugar
3 tablespoons Sherry or
Madeira
2 dl (3/4 cup) whipping
cream
2 dl (3/4 cup) preserved
cherries or cherry compote

Bring milk and salt to a boil. Add barley and simmer over low heat about one hour. Cool. Toast nuts and rub off skins. Grind. Stir sugar, wine and nuts into barley mixture. Whip cream and fold into barley mixture. Spoon into individual dishes and top with cherries.

BEVERAGE SUGGESTION:
This dessert really does not need any drink. If desired, a hearty or fruity fortified wine from South Africa, made with Muscat grapes, can be served with this rather filling dessert.

Honey-grilled, lightly salted ham with warm apple salad and potato gratin with horseradish

THIRD PRIZE
IN THE COOKBOOK COMPETITION
FESTIVE MENUS

JOAKIM FUNK
KARSTORPS KONFERENS CENTER, SKÖVDE

KARSTORP CONFERENCE CENTER is right in the middle of the countryside, yet it is only a few kilometers from the city. Chef Joakim Funk gets plump crayfish for his appetizer from Karstorp Lake and nearby streams. It is also natural for him to use local cheeses. "Our regional cheeses are full of flavor," he says. He also likes to use tender Swedish lamb. He feels that we eat too little of it.

All recipes serve four.

Appetizer
MANGOLD AND CHEESE PANCAKES
WITH CRAYFISH TAILS
AND GOLDEN CAVIAR SAUCE

Main dish
GARLIC AND HERB ROASTED
RACK OF LAMB
WITH POTATO TERRINE, WAX BEANS,
ASPARAGUS AND CHANTERELLE JUS

Dessert
RASPBERRY SOUP WITH
VANILLA-MINT BAVARIAN CREAM
AND LEMON MUFFINS

Mangold and cheese pancakes with crayfish tails and golden caviar sauce

Pancakes:
1 egg
6 tablespoons flour
2 dl (3/4 cup) light cream
20 g (3 tablespoons) grated cheese
1/2 teaspoon salt
35 g (1 oz) mangold
15 g (2 tablespoons) chopped onion
butter

Golden caviar sauce:
2 tablespoons whipping cream
2 tablespoons sour cream
1 tablespoon golden caviar
2 teaspoons chopped red onion
2 teaspoons chopped dill
salt and pepper

12-16 freshwater crayfish tails or
8-12 ocean crayfish tails
dill

PANCAKES:
Whisk together egg, flour, and cream, then add cheese and salt. Let rest at least 30 minutes. Sauté mangold and onion lightly in butter. Cool, then stir into batter. Make 12 small pancakes.

GOLDEN CAVIAR SAUCE:
Combine cream and sour cream. Drain caviar and add with red onion and dill. Season with salt and pepper.
To serve, arrange three pancakes on each plate. Top with crayfish and garnish with a dill frond. Drizzle sauce all around.

BEVERAGE SUGGESTION: A dry white wine made from Sauvignon Blanc grapes, preferably a crisp Sancerre or Pouilly Fumé, is best with this dish.

Garlic and herb roasted rack of lamb with potato terrine, wax beans, asparagus and chanterelle jus

Potato terrine:
600 g (1 1/3 lb) potatoes
1/2 dl (3 1/2 tablespoons)
light cream
1 garlic clove, chopped
1 bay leaf, crushed
1/8 teaspoon ground nutmeg
1/8 teaspoon cayenne pepper
salt and pepper

Rack of lamb:
720 g (1 2/3 lb) rack of lamb
salt and pepper
2 tablespoons each chopped thyme,
coriander and basil
3 garlic cloves
2 tablespoons olive oil

Chanterelle jus:
1 small onion
160 g (6 oz) blanched chanterelles
butter
4 dl (1 2/3 cups) lamb stock
1 dl (1/2 cup) red wine
salt and pepper

Preserved wax beans and asparagus:
100 g (4 oz) wax beans
100 g (4 oz) asparagus
1/2 tablespoon butter
1/2 tablespoon dark corn syrup
1/2 tablespoon
apple cider vinegar
salt and pepper

POTATO TERRINE:
Preheat oven to 175°C (350°F). Peel and thinly slice potatoes. Do not rinse. Combine all ingredients and pour into a rectangular form. Press down well with a spatula. Bake 25-30 minutes. Reduce temperature to 150°C (300°F), then bake 25-30 minutes more. Press potatoes down several times while baking. Cool slightly. Loosen with a knife and unmold. Cut into serving portions.

RACK OF LAMB
Preheat oven to 175°C (350°F). Cut lamb into four pieces of equal size. Trim bones, saving trimmings for stock. Score fat. Brown meat, then season with salt and pepper. Puree herbs, garlic and oil in a food processor. Brush meat with the mixture. Roast 10-15 minutes.

CHANTERELLE JUS:
Mince onion and sauté in butter with chanterelles. Add stock and red wine. Reduce until about half of the original amount remains. If sauce is too thin, thicken with a teaspoon of cornstarch stirred into a tablespoon of cold water.

WAX BEANS AND ASPARAGUS:
Clean vegetables and cut into bite-size pieces. Blanch in boiling water. Sauté vegetables in butter and syrup. Stir in vinegar and season with salt and pepper. Arrange a slice of potato terrine on each plate. Top with lamb. Sprinkle vegetables all around. Spoon jus all around. Garnish with thyme.

BEVERAGE SUGGESTION: Rack of lamb with herbs, garlic and flavorful side dishes goes well with a cask-aged full-bodied red wine, such as a Crianza or Reserva from Rioja or Valdepeñas in Spain.

Raspberry soup with vanilla-mint bavarian cream and lemon muffins

Vanilla-mint bavarian cream:
6 tablespoons whipping cream
6 tablespoons light cream
3 tablespoons sugar
1/5 vanilla bean,
split lengthwise
1 gelatin sheet
6 tablespoons natural yogurt
2 mint leaves, finely chopped

Lemon muffins:
125 g (4 oz) butter
grated rind of 1/2 lemon
2 dl (2/3 cup) sugar
2 eggs
3 dl (1 1/4 cups) flour
1 teaspoon baking powder
juice of 1 lemon

Raspberry soup:
1/4 vanilla bean,
split lengthwise
2 1/2 dl (1 cup) water
1/2 dl (3 1/2 tablespoons) sugar
3 1/2 dl (1 1/2 cups) raspberries

VANILLA-MINT BAVARIAN CREAM:
Scald cream and sugar with vanilla bean. Soak gelatin sheet in cold water to soften about 10 minutes. Squeeze excess water from gelatin sheet and melt in hot cream. Remove vanilla bean. Stir in yogurt and mint. Pour into four individual custard cups and refrigerate at least three hours.

LEMON MUFFINS:
Preheat oven to 200°C (400°F). Beat butter, lemon rind and sugar until light and fluffy. Add eggs, one at a time, beating well after each. Combine flour and baking powder and add alternately with the lemon juice. Pour into greased miniature muffin tins and bake about 10 minutes. Makes about 20 muffins. These muffins freeze well.

RASPBERRY SOUP:
Bring vanilla bean, water and sugar to a boil. Cool. Remove vanilla bean, then pour into a food processor with raspberries and puree. Strain, discarding tiny seeds. Divide soup among four deep dishes or soup bowls. Place a bavarian cream and a muffin in each. Garnish with mint leaves.

BEVERAGE SUGGESTION: A dessert soup does not need a drink, but if desired, a light, sweet fortified wine from Muscat grapes is a good accompaniment. Good wines of this type are made all along the northern Mediterranean coast.

GARLIC AND HERB ROASTED RACK OF LAMB WITH POTATO TERRINE, WAX BEANS, ASPARAGUS AND CHANTERELLE JUS

RICKARD HALLERÖD
RONNUMS HERRGÅRD

RICKARD HALLERÖD HAS BEEN at beautiful Ronnum Manor for 14 years and has helped to make it into a modern conference center with a top class restaurant. "I have a strong emotional attachment to Ronnum," he says. It is still a very creative and developing place. He has chosen ingredients with a local connection for his menu. There is a lot of moose around here, especially during hunting season. According to Rickard, pike-perch is the best freshwater fish. It is easy to bone and can be prepared in many ways.

All recipes serve four.

Appetizer
MOOSE CARPACCIO
WITH GRATED SPIKED CHEESE AND
LINGONBERRY COMPOTE

Main dish
GRILLED FILLET OF PIKE-PERCH WITH
CHANTERELLE POTATOES,
WARM BLACK SALSIFY SALAD AND
ROSEMARY BEURRE BLANC

Dessert
WARM APPLE SOUP
WITH CINNAMON AND HONEY,
SERVED WITH A TERRINE
OF VANILLA ICE CREAM

Moose carpaccio with grated spiked cheese and lingonberry compote

280 g (10 oz) strip loin or filet of moose
fleur de sel gourmet salt
freshly ground black pepper
rapeseed oil
1/2 dl (3 1/2 tablespoons) lingonberries
1 tablespoon honey
1/2 red onion, chopped
fresh thyme
100 g (3 1/2 oz) aquavit-spiked cheese

Freeze moose. Defrost slightly and slice as thinly as possible. Brush lightly with oil and sprinkle with salt and pepper. Simmer lingonberries, onion and honey a few minutes. Season with salt, pepper and chopped fresh thyme. Cool. Arrange the meat on individual plates. Coarsely grate cheese and sprinkle over meat. Spoon lingonberries in the center. Serve immediately with crusty bread.

BEVERAGE SUGGESTION:
This appetizer features traditional Swedish ingredients. Serve a glass of beer, preferably a dark ale from one of the new Swedish small breweries.

Grilled pike-perch with chanterelle potatoes, warm black salsify salad and rosemary beurre blanc

*640 g (1 1/2 lb) pike-perch
fillets
coarse salt and white pepper
8 potatoes
1 dl (1/2 cup) blanched
chanterelles or other wild
mushrooms
1/2 leek, minced
butter
1/2 small onion, minced
1 twig rosemary
2 dl (3/4 cup) dry white wine
2 dl (3/4 cup) fish stock
2 dl (3/4 cup) whipping cream
50 g (3 tablespoons)
unsalted butter
3 black salsify
olive oil
1-2 teaspoons red wine vinegar
2 tablespoons chopped chives*

Trim fillets and remove all bones with a tweezers. Sprinkle with salt and refrigerate. Peel potatoes and boil until tender. Sauté chanterelles and leek in a little butter. In another pan, sauté onion in a little butter. Add a few rosemary leaves, then add wine and stock and simmer 5-10 minutes. Add cream and reduce until about two-thirds of the original amount remains. Transfer to a food processor, add butter and puree until smooth. Season with salt and pepper. Peel black salsify and cut into diagonal slices. Sauté in olive oil until crisp-tender. Add vinegar and chopped chives. Season with salt and pepper.

Just before serving, mash potatoes, leaving a few lumps. Stir in chanterelles and a pat of butter. Season with salt and pepper. Pack potato mixture into rings or well-buttered cups.

Heat a grill pan. Pour in a film of oil and a little salt. Grill fish, skin-side down, two minutes per side. Cover and let rest a few minutes.

To serve, unmold the potatoes on individual plates. Serve fish with salsify salad and rosemary sauce.

BEVERAGE SUGGESTION: The slightly burnt flavor of the fish is good with a cask-aged white wine, preferably one from Rioja or Penedes in northern Spain.

Warm apple soup with cinnamon and honey, served with a terrine of vanilla ice cream

*1 vanilla bean, split
lengthwise
1/2 dl (3 1/2 tablespoons) sugar
2 tablespoons water
3 dl (1 1/4 cups) light cream
3 egg yolks
4 large apples
2 dl (3/4 cup) white wine
2-4 tablespoons honey
2 cinnamon sticks*

Bring vanilla, sugar and water to a boil. Cool slightly. Whip cream and refrigerate. Whisk egg yolks in a bowl placed over hot water. Remove vanilla bean from syrup and add, whisking constantly. Cool, then fold in cream. Pour into a small loaf pan. Freeze at least four hours.

Peel and core apples. Cook in a saucepan with wine, honey and cinnamon. If mixture starts to dry out, add a little water. When apples are soft, remove cinnamon sticks and press mixture through a food mill into another saucepan. Reheat and season to taste with a little more wine, sugar and cinnamon, if desired. Serve the soup warm with a thick slice of ice cream terrine.

BEVERAGE SUGGESTION: It is difficult to match a wine with this soup, but Tokay is probably the best choice in this case.

GRILLED PIKE-PERCH WITH CHANTERELLE POTATOES, WARM BLACK SALSIFY SALAD AND ROSEMARY BEURRE BLANC

STEFAN GRYNGE
RESTAURANGSKOLAN LYON
SKÖVDE

According to Stefan Grynge, who has done a lot of research on food and traditions, cheese soup was a way of using up old bread and whey, the byproduct of cheese production. Eggs and cream were added on festive occasions.

Salmon was poor man's food during the 1700s and 1800s. Trout had a higher status, and pike, perch and burbot were even more prized. Flour was never used in sauces. Mashed vegetables and fruit were mixed with liquid to make puree sauces.

These sour cream pancakes may have been invented by Kajsa Warg, and there were plenty of wild strawberries around Skaraborg during the 1700s. Wild strawberries were botanist Linnaeus' favorite food. He thought they could cure his gout.

Here is Stefan Grynge's 18th century menu prepared with ingredients available today.

All recipes serve four.

Appetizer
SKARABORG CHEESE SOUP

❧

Main dish
SAUTÉED COLD-SMOKED TROUT
FROM VÄTTERN WITH DILL-FLAVORED
LEEKS AND POTATOES AND
CREAMY GREEN ASPARAGUS SAUCE

❧

Dessert
SOUR CREAM PANCAKES WITH WHIPPED
CREAM AND WILD STRAWBERRY SAUCE

Skaraborg cheese soup

40 g (2 1/2 tablespoons) butter
2 tablespoons flour
1 liter (4 cups) veal stock
6 dl (2 1/2cups) grated Swiss cheese
(preferably a rather dry, aged variety)
4 dl (1 2/3 cups) light cream
2 raw eggs
6 cl (1/4 cup) cherry wine
1 1/2 tablespoons kirsch or
pure grain alcohol
4 hard-cooked eggs
salt

Melt butter in a large saucepan and stir in flour. Gradually whisk in stock and simmer until sooth. Add cheese and cream and bring to a boil. Stir as little as possible so cheese won't become stringy. Whisk raw eggs, wine and kirsch together, then whisk carefully into soup. Simmer a few minutes.

Coarsely chop eggs and carefully stir into soup. Add a little salt, if necessary.

Serve with toast topped with grated cheese.

BEVERAGE SUGGESTION: This soup is quite similar to cheese fondue, so it seems natural to do as the Swiss and serve a dry white wine, preferably from Alsace, Greece or Portugal.

Sautéed cold-smoked trout from Vättern with dill-flavored leeks and potatoes and creamy green asparagus sauce

Potatoes:
500 g (1 1/4 lb) potatoes
100 g (4 oz) leek
4 dl (1 2/3 cups) fish stock
4-5 tablespoons chopped dill

Sauce:
*150 g (5 oz) tiny green asparagus
or tips from larger asparagus*
1/2 small onion
butter
1 dl (1/2 cup) concentrated fish stock
salt
2 dl (1 cup) whipping cream
*400 g (14 oz) cold-smoked
fillet of trout*

Peel and slice potatoes. Shred leek. Add to stock and simmer about 10 minutes. Drain, reserving stock for the sauce. Just before serving, fold in chopped dill.

Finely chop asparagus and onion. Sauté onion in butter until shiny, then add asparagus, stock and a little salt. Bring to a boil. Add cream and reduce until about two-thirds of the original amount remains. Pour into a food processor and puree until smooth. Season with salt, if desired.

Cut fish into small, thin slices and brown quickly in butter.

BEVERAGE SUGGESTION: The hearty flavor of the smoked fish demands a full-bodied, dry white wine. A green Veltliner (preferably of Emerald quality) from Austria is recommended.

Sour cream pancakes with whipped cream and wild strawberry sauce

Pancakes:
*1 1/2 dl (2/3 cup) crème fraiche or
natural sour cream (do not use low-fat)*
1 1/2 dl (2/3 cup) flour
1 teaspoon baking powder
1/2 dl (3 1/2 tablespoons) sugar
1/4 teaspoon vanilla extract
butter

Wild strawberry sauce:
1 1/2 dl (2/3 cup) light cream
*200 g (7-8 oz) wild or
domestic strawberries*
1 dl (scant 1/2 cup) sugar

Combine pancake ingredients and let rest about 30 minutes. Fry small round pancakes in butter on a hot griddle.

Puree cream, strawberries and sugar in a food processor until smooth. Serve with whipped cream.

BEVERAGE SUGGESTION:
These pancakes with strawberries and cream are even more heavenly with a glass of sweet Bordeaux or for an even more festive drink, Sauternes.

SAUTÉED COLD-SMOKED TROUT FROM VÄTTERN WITH DILL-FLAVORED LEEKS
AND POTATOES AND CREAMY GREEN ASPARAGUS SAUCE

MARTIN LUNDGREN
VITA HUSET I KINNA

AT THE APPROPRIATELY NAMED "White House" in Kinna, the menu is inspired by the cuisine of that great nation across the sea. Both interior and food are American and the wines are chiefly from California. But when chef Martin Lundgren relaxes, he reaches for 100% Swedish ingredients such as perch. And his favorite meats are roe deer and lamb.

"Roe deer has a lovely gamy flavor, and the meat is always tender," he says. For the finale, he likes a classic dessert, in this case, a soufflé with blueberries and a parfait with Swedish punsch liqueur.

All recipes serve four.

Appetizer
GRILLED PERCH ON A BED
OF MANGOLD AND ARUGULA WITH BEETS
AND HORSERADISH

❧

Main dish
ROE DEER WITH SWEET POTATO GRATIN,
CREAMED CÈPES,
PEAR CHUTNEY AND MILD PEPPER JUS

❧

Dessert
LEMON-BLUEBERRY SOUFFLÉ
WITH PUNSCH PARFAIT

Grilled perch on a bed of mangold and arugula with beets and horseradish

2 beets
juice of 2 lemons
1 dl (scant 1/2 cup) rapeseed
or corn oil
salt and pepper
100 g (3 1/2 oz) horseradish
1 tablespoon cornstarch
oil
400 g (14 oz) boneless perch fillets,
scaled but skin-on
100 g (3 1/2 oz) arugula
100 g (3 1/2 oz mangold
or 200 g (7 oz) mixed delicate salad
greens

Peel and thinly slice beets with a cheese plane. Combine lemon juice, oil, salt and pepper and pour over beets. Marinate at least 1 hour. Cut 3/4 of the horseradish into matchstick Pieces. Toss in cornstarch and deepfry until golden brown. Salt lightly.
Grill fish, skin side down, in a hot grill pan. Turn and grill until heated through. Heat some of the marinade. Grate remaining horseradish and toss with arugula and mangold. Drizzle with marinade. Divide the salad among individual serving plates. Top with fish. Garnish with beets and fried horseradish.

BEVERAGE
SUGGESTION:
A dry white wine or even better, a fresh rosé from Spain or the south of France goes well with this perch on its bed of summer vegetables.

Roe deer with sweet potato gratin, creamed cèpes, pear chutney and mild pepper jus

Mild pepper jus:
Bones and trimmings from
roe deer roast
1/2 head of garlic
3 carrots
1 small chunk celeriac
2 parsnips
3 medium onions
1 beef bouillon cube
1 bay leaf
10 white peppercorns
several juniper berries
rosemary and thyme
3 3/4 dl (1 1/2 cups) red wine
sugar
red wine vinegar
1 heaping tablespoon crushed
white peppercorns
25 g (2 tablespoons) unsalted butter

Sweet potato gratin:
4 baking potatoes
4 sweet potatoes
2 garlic cloves, minced
salt and pepper
6 dl (2 1/2 cups) light cream

Pear chutney:
2 pears
1 small chile
1 garlic clove
1 small chunk ginger
1 cinnamon stick
1 pinch ground cloves
1 dl (scant 1/2 cup) sugar
2 tablespoons apple cider vinegar

Roe deer roast:
800 g (1 3/4 lb) boneless roe deer roast
1 teaspoon thyme
1 bay leaf
oil
salt and peppe

Creamed cèpes:
250 g (8 oz) cèpes or other mushrooms
1 dl (1/3 cup) whipping cream
salt and pepper

Jus:

Preheat oven to 200°C (400°F). Place bones and root vegetables in an oiled oven tray and roast until browned, about 30 minutes. Turn over halfway through cooking time. Transfer to a large saucepan and add water just to cover, bouillon cube and seasonings. Simmer about 3 hours. Strain. Add red wine and reduce until about 3 dl (1 1/4 cups) remain. Season to taste with sugar and red wine vinegar. Just before serving, add crushed peppercorns. Boil 30 seconds, then strain and discard the peppercorns. This gives the jus a rich pepper aroma without making it too strong. Whisk in butter, but do not allow to boil.

Sweet potato gratin:

Preheat oven to 175°C (350°F). Peel and slice potatoes with a cheese plane. Layer in a greased ovenproof dish, sprinkling each layer with garlic, salt and pepper. The layers should be no more than 5 cm (2") high. Pour over cream. It should just reach the top of the potatoes. Bake about 1 hour, until potatoes are tender. Press the potatoes down lightly with a spatula about halfway through cooking time.

Pear chutney:

Peel and cube pears and place in a saucepan. Mince chile, garlic and ginger and add with spices. Cook slowly over low heat until pears are soft. Add sugar and vinegar and cook a few more minutes.

Roe deer roast:

Preheat oven to 175°C (350°F). Roll meat and tie, if necessary. Crush herbs and rub into meat. Brown on all sides in hot oil. Season with salt and pepper. Roast until internal temperature reaches 65°C (140°F). Roasting time varies according to dimensions of the roast. Start checking after 15-20 minutes. A long, thin roast could take even less time. Wrap in aluminum foil and let rest for at least 10 minutes before serving.

Creamed cèpes:

Clean and cube mushrooms. Sauté without added fat a few minutes, then add cream and reduce to desired consistency. Season with salt and pepper.

Beverage suggestion:

A light, fruity red wine works well with the mild gaminess of the roe deer and the nutty sweetness of the potatoes. A wine made with Merlot grapes, with their tendency toward sweetness, is especially good. Alternatives from Italy, Chile and California can be found in all price ranges.

ROE DEER WITH SWEET POTATO GRATIN, CREAMED CÈPES, PEAR CHUTNEY AND MILD PEPPER JUS

Blueberry-lemon soufflé with punsch parfait

Punsch parfait:
1/2 dl (3 1/2 tablespoons)
crushed amaretti biscuits
1/2 dl (3 1/2 tablespoons)
Swedish punsch liqueur
5 egg yolks
100 g (2/3 cup) confectioner's sugar
1/2 teaspoon vanilla extract
5 dl (2 cups) whipping cream

Soufflé:
6 egg, separated
60 g (1/2 cup) flour
5 dl (2 cups) coffee cream
or half and half
grated rind and juice of 1 lemon
150 g (1 1/2 cups) blueberries
3 tablespoons cornstarch
4 tablespoons (1/4 cup) sugar

PARFAIT:
Soak biscuits in punsch. Beat egg yolks, confectioner's sugar and vanilla until light and lemon-colored. Fold in biscuit mixture. Whip cream and fold into egg yolk mixture. Pour into a mold lined with plastic wrap. Freeze at least 4 hours.

SOUFFLÉ:
Preheat oven to 200°C (400°F). Butter and sugar a soufflé form. Combine egg yolks, flour and half the cream. Scald remaining cream and whisk into egg yolk mixture. Whisk in lemon rind, juice and cornstarch. Fold in berries. Beat egg whites until almost stiff. Add sugar and beat until stiff but not dry. Fold into soufflé mixture. Pour into prepared form. Bake on lowest oven shelf until it is risen and golden, about 30 minutes. Serve with a thin blueberry sauce made from fresh or frozen blueberries, sugar and vanilla. This dessert serves 6.

BEVERAGE SUGGESTION: What is more natural than to serve a small glass of chilled punsch with this dessert? A sweet and freshBeerenauslese from Austria is good choice for those who prefer wine.

CHRISTER FALKHOLT
FALKHOLTS GESTGIFVERI
DALS LÅNGED

BEAVER, IS IT REALLY EDIBLE? "Yes, it tastes great," assures Christer Falkholt. Beaver resembles hare in flavor, but it is a bit gamier. Christer runs Falkholts Gestgifveri (Inn) in Dals Långed. It used to be an old school building from 1905, but the old classroom is the dining room now. He serves dishes utilizing fish and game, berries and mushrooms from the woods and lakes nearby, which he turns into delicacies. The beaver was eradicated in Sweden at the end of the last century, but it was reintroduced around 1920. Since that time, the beaver population has increased greatly. If it is impossible to obtain beaver, serve another kind of smoked meat with the avocado-cottage cheese salad.

All recipes serve four.

Appetizer
SMOKED BEAVER ON A BED
OF AVOCADO-COTTAGE CHEESE SALAD

Main dish
PIKE BURGERS
WITH HERB CREAM SAUCE

Dessert
RHUBARB CONSOMMÉ WITH
FRESH BERRIES

Smoked beaver on a bed of avocado-cottage cheese salad

2 avocados
2 1/2 dl (1 cup) cottage cheese
1 teaspoon Dijon-style mustard
freshly grated horseradish
salt and pepper
300 g (10 oz) smoked beaver or other smoked meat, thinly sliced
1 tomato, peeled, seeded and diced
fresh thyme

Halve avocados and discard pit. Scoop out flesh and mash. Combine with cottage cheese, mustard, horseradish, salt and pepper. Divide among four individual plates. Top with slices of smoked beaver. Garnish with diced tomato and fresh thyme.

BEVERAGE SUGGESTION: The salty richness of smoked meat needs a wine with some contrast, such as a light red or a semi-dry white wine.

Pike burgers with herb cream sauce
recipe page 52

Pike burgers with herb cream sauce

*About 500 g (1 1/4 lb) skinless and
boneless pike fillets
Salt and pepper
a few drops Tabasco sauce
pinch sweet paprika
2 1/2 dl (1 cup) light cream
3 eggs
125 g (4 1/2 oz) blanched spinach leaves
(if using frozen, remove as much water
as possible before measuring)
50 g (1 3/4 oz) smoked salmon
1 dl (scant 1/2 cup) blanched chanterelles
butter*

*Herb cream sauce:
2 shallots, chopped
corn oil
2 dl (3/4 cup) white wine
3 dl (1 1/4 cups) unsalted fish stock
2 dl (3/4 cup) whipping cream
1 teaspoon cornstarch stirred into
2 teaspoons water (optional)
1 teaspoon Dijon-style mustard
salt and pepper
1 dl (scant 1/2 cup) chopped fresh herbs,
such as parsley, dill, chives
chopped chives*

Cut the fish into chunks and place in a food processor. With the motor running, add seasonings, cream and eggs, one at a time. Press through a sieve. Chop spinach, salmon and mushrooms and add to the fish. Form into burgers and fry in butter. Leftover burgers are good cold in sandwiches! For the sauce, sweat shallot in a little oil. Add wine and reduce until half the original amount remains. Add fish stock and reduce by half. Add cream and reduce by half once more. Thicken with cornstarch, if desired. Season with mustard, salt and pepper. Transfer to a food processor and puree until smooth. Stir in herbs. Spoon a mirror of sauce onto each plate. Top with burgers. Garnish with chopped chives. Serve with boiled potatoes.

BEVERAGE SUGGESTION: This is a classic fish dish, which goes well with most dry white wines. With spinach and smoked salmon in the sauce, a Sauvignon Blanc, preferably from Sancerre, is the best choice.

Rhubarb consommé with fresh berries

*about 1 liter (4 cups)
rhubarb, unpeeled,
in chunks
about 3 dl
(1 1/2 cups) sugar
fresh berries in season*

Simmer rhubarb with sugar and a little water until tender. Drain through a sieve. Do not press down. Cool. Serve consommé in soup bowls with berries, preferably blueberries and strawberries, and a scoop of ice cream.

BEVERAGE SUGGESTION: With its slightly sour flavor, rhubarb is best on its own. If you must have a sweet wine, it should be quite robust, such as a Tokay 5 puttonyos.

HORNBORGASJÖN

Rhubarb consommé with fresh berries

GÖTE WESTERBERG
GÖTES FESTVÅNING, LIDKÖPING

Götes Festvåning (banquet hall) is in Lidköping's old town and overlooks Lidan as well as Magnus Gabriel's hunting lodge on the square. Many weddings have been held in this locale over the years. It has also been known as Inga's dining rooms and the Lundgren sisters' dining rooms.

Now they are named after Göte Westerberg. Göte gets salmon for this spring menu from a smokehouse in Lidköping. The quail eggs come from small local producers. And veal is the perfect main dish.

"Believe it or not, the people of this area consume the most meat in Sweden," says Göte.

All recipes serve four.

Appetizer
SMOKED SALMON PACKETS WITH SPINACH AND POACHED QUAIL EGGS

Main dish
FILET OF VEAL WITH ASPARAGUS, SNOW PEAS, TURNIPS, TINY POTATOES AND MADEIRA SAUCE

Dessert
SPRING TOWER WITH GINGER CREAM

Smoked salmon packets with spinach and poached quail eggs

8 quail eggs
vinegar
250 g (8 oz) frozen or 500 g (1 lb) fresh spinach
butter
3 dl (1 1/4 cups) whipping cream
salt and pepper
4 slices smoked salmon, about 80 g (3 oz) each
2 tablespoons Greek-style natural yogurt
chopped chives

Poach eggs 1-2 minutes in lightly salted water with a little vinegar. Transfer to lukewarm water and reserve. Rinse and blanch fresh spinach. Squeeze excess water from both frozen or fresh spinach. Sauté in butter, then add a third of the cream and cook a few minutes, until thickened. Season with salt and pepper.

Spread out salmon slices. Top with spinach and eggs. Fold into a packet. Place on individual plates, seam side down. Reduce remaining cream until half the original amount remains. Stir in yogurt. Drizzle sauce around salmon packets. Garnish with chives.

BEVERAGE SUGGESTION: A light and fresh, dry white wine is best with these salmon packets, with their lovely flavor of fresh spinach. Even a glass of sparkling wine is good with this dish.

FILET OF VEAL WITH ASPARAGUS, SNOW PEAS, TURNIPS,
TINY POTATOES AND MADEIRA SAUCE
RECIPE PAGE 56

Filet of veal with asparagus, snow peas, turnips, tiny potatoes and Madeira sauce

8 stalks white asparagus
8 stalks green asparagus
200 g (8 oz) baby turnips
butter
salt, pepper and sugar
800 g (1 3/4 lb) filet of veal
800 g (1 3/4 lb) new potatoes
5 dl (2 cups) veal stock
2 dl (3/4 cup) Madeira
100 g (4 oz) snow peas
chopped fresh dill

Pare white asparagus stalks. Cook asparagus separately until crisp-tender. Set aside. Peel turnips and cut into wedges. Steam, covered, in 1 tablespoon butter and 1 tablespoon water. Season with salt, pepper and sugar.

Preheat oven to 175°C (350°F). Trim and tie veal. Season and brown on all sides in butter. Roast until internal temperature reaches 65-70°C (140-158°F), about 20 minutes. Wrap meat in aluminum foil and let rest about 10 minutes before serving. Brush potatoes. Brown in butter, then roast with meat until done, about 15-20 minutes.

While meat is roasting, combine stock and Madeira and reduce over high heat until about half the original amount remains. Cook until syrupy. Just before serving, beat in 1-2 tablespoons butter. Do not allow sauce to boil after butter has been added. Blanch snow peas in lightly salted water. Cut into diagonal slices. To serve, cut meat into thin slices and arrange with turnips. Top with asparagus. Sprinkle with snow peas. Halve potatoes, then coat with butter and dill. Drizzle sauce all around. Serve remaining sauce alongside.

BEVERAGE SUGGESTION: A medium-bodied, fruity red wine with some tannin enhances the flavor of the veal. Try a Chianti, a light Bordeaux or a vine from the Loire Valley.

Spring tower with ginger cream

300 g (10 oz) rhubarb
1 dl (1/3 cup light corn syrup
1/2 teaspoon grated ginger
2 gelatin sheets

Almond snaps:
50 g (1/2 cup) chopped almonds
1/2 dl (3 1/2 tablespoons) sugar
50 g (3 1/2 tablespoons) butter
1 tablespoon flour
1 teaspoon light corn syrup

Grand Marnier zabaglione:
1 gelatin sheet
2 dl (3/4cup) white wine
120 g (2/3 cup) sugar
4 egg yolks
3 tablespoons Grand Marnier

Ginger cream:
1 gelatin sheet
100 g (3 oz) fresh ginger
1 dl (1/3 cup) sugar
1 dl (1/3 cup) water
1 1/2 dl (2/3 cup) whipping cream

1 small punnet strawberries

Peel the rhubarb and cut into 1 cm lengths. Steam, covered, with syrup, 1 tablespoon water and the grated ginger, until tender. While the rhubarb is steaming, soak the gelatin sheets in cold water to soften, about 10 minutes. Squeeze excess water from gelatin sheets and melt in hot rhubarb mixture. Divide among four cups and refrigerate until set, at least two hours.

Preheat the oven to 175°C (350°F). Combine all ingredients for almond snaps in a saucepan over low heat. Spoon onto a greased and floured cookie sheet. Bake until bubbly, about 8 minutes. Transfer immediately to a rack to cool.

Follow above procedure for gelatin. Combine wine, sugar and egg yolks in a saucepan. Whisk over low heat until thick. Melt gelatin in the wine mixture. Stir in the liqueur. Remove from the heat and stir until cool. Refrigerate. Follow above procedure for gelatin. Chop the ginger and cook with sugar and water until it disintegrates. Melt gelatin in hot ginger mixture. Cool. Whip the cream and mix with the ginger puree.

To serve, unmold the rhubarb on each plate. Build a tower with almond snaps, zabaglione, sliced strawberries, ending with an almond snap. Pipe ginger cream on top and decorate with more strawberries.

BEVERAGE SUGGESTION: Even the youngest rhubarb is too sour for wine. But with the almond snaps and zabaglione to temper the flavor, a glass of well chilled Asti Spumante is just the thing with this spring dessert.

SPRING TOWER WITH GINGER CREAM

"Come to Bohuslän and taste egg-cheese!"

THE FIRST TIME I heard the name, I decided never to try this strange dish. Egg-cheese! Good grief! It doesn't sound at all delicious, for an east Swede, like me. Egg-cheese! Just taste the name – egg with cheese! Can it possibly be good?

But it is perfectly clear – if you move to Bohuslän with its cliffs, its farms, its greenery, its strawberries, its potatoes, its water, its shellfish, its fish, its mussels, its egg-cheese...

There it comes again. Egg-cheese! Good heavens, what is it really?

I live on the island of Åstol. Here you have to eat egg-cheese. Everyone eats egg-cheese. All the ladies can make egg-cheese. It's inherited. It's in their genes.

And those who don't happen to have it in their genes, because they moved here from somewhere else—they just have to learn to make egg-cheese.

We hadn't lived on the island more than a month when we saw a note posted in a shop. It said:

"Learn how to make Egg-cheese."

Yes, that was how it was written, capital "E" and all.

My wife, who has always been very brave about trying new kinds of food and drink, saw the note and made up her mind. Now she would learn how to make...egg-cheese.

I remember how old men in Normandy looked with wide eyes and wonderment at this little Swedish woman when, despite warnings from other diners and waiters alike, she wolfed down tripe with Calvados with gusto.

And I haven't forgotten the old Scots in the Hebrides, who got tears in their eyes as they watched her wash her crab sandwich down with a small, smoky malt from Islay. (If you ask me, I think it was like rubbing your tongue on a tarbrush.)

Of course, my wife would learn to make egg-cheese. She absolutely adores local specialties.

Thanks, many thanks, a thousand thanks, to Mrs. Runegrund, who taught my Lotta the trick, indeed the art, of making egg-cheese. Otherwise, I would never have tasted this wonderful food.

The nice thing is that it can be eaten as an appetizer, with herring, and as a dessert, when sugared, or with blackberry jam.

At the same time, I also found out what those strange molds are used for.

I had seen them not only in people's homes, but at every auction in Bohuslän.

So don't hesitate, you weak souls.

Come to Bohuslän! Come out to the islands, to the sea and the free! But above all else – come and taste the EGG-CHEESE!

Peter Harryson

"Read books and eat fish"

I GREW UP IN ÖRGRYTE, a neighborhood in Gothenburg. We used to shop at our local grocery, owned by a rather stern looking man named Gustafsson, who had colorless hair and wore a white coat and a yellow pencil behind his ear. In 1950, he announced with a smile that he was now selling frozen fish, and that customers' children would get five cents for each bone found in these frozen fillets.

That was one of Findus' early marketing campaigns. I was six years old and didn't understand a thing. Nobody I knew was afraid of a fishbone. Turning a whole fried plaice with a fork and knife was as easy as pie. What was the point of boneless fish? The next steps would surely be hens without carcasses, porridge without almonds, and pork ribs without crackling.

During the summer, I used to go fishing at sunset with my uncle Harald near the island of Vinga. The boats were so close together that we could talk to one another. Everyone got a bite at the same time – mostly whiting, sometimes flounder. We waved to *Patricia*, sailing for London, and to *Kungsholm* and *Gripsholm* bound for America. Kitchen workers threw fish guts and shrimp shells overboard, and the gulls would hover all the way to New York.

My uncle cleaned the fish onboard, and I cast a line for mackerel on the way home. Aunt Alice fried the whiting until it curled, and we ate it cold for breakfast the next day – delicious, but with lots of bones. During the day, we sailed and went ashore on

different skerries with our shrimp-nets in tow. We cooked shrimp and small crabs in sea water, and ate them with the shells on. Sometimes, we grilled mussels.

My father, Hubert, used to sketch the salty old boys in Gothenburg's fish harbor on auction day. Sometimes, I went with him at dawn, on the frame of his blue bicycle. The fish auction was an interesting adventure. Mysterious blinks and the silver of the sea. Lumpfish, monkfish, catfish, spiny dogfish – exciting names, and many different flavors. "Fish fishermen fish for fish, but herring and mackerel are fish, too," said a fisherman on the radio. We listened to the fish harbor report, which was certainly more interesting than the poem of the day.

But speaking of poetry, the most poetic fish is the mackerel. The first mackerel caught in the spring sings far better than any lark. My mother Katarina was an excellent cook. Friends made pilgrimages to us for a taste of her fried spring mackerel, boiled potatoes with dill, fresh spinach, beer and a little glass of something strong – which was always filled with Harald Jensen's schnapps because it tasted so good, and because a percentage of the profits went to poor children in Denmark.

Katarina also created the most beautiful and delicious seafood platters. Once during the 1970s, Floyd Patterson was able to relax and enjoy her seafood salad, even though Ingemar Johansson sat facing him across the table. Whenever she was in a restaurant, my mother threw withering glances at the wedges of boiled egg, which sometimes popped up among the shrimp and crab-claws in the seafood salad. "Which sea has this egg been swimming in?" she would ask the waiter.

During recent summers, it has almost been possible to catch mackerel with bare hands in Lysekil. Tourists and retired fishermen, young mothers, boat refugees with bamboo rods stand along the quays. And menus listing at least twenty different ways to prepare mackerel are posted at the entrance to all the restaurants. But still, simplest is best. With bones. Poor grocer Gustafsson. I don't think he ever swallowed that bait of five cents per fishbone.

Now and then I receive letters with questions from children who read my books. How do you become an author?

I usually answer: Read books and eat fish.

Viveca Lärn

The strange struggle at Kvistrum

THE NEXT-TO-THE-LAST TIME any form of organized combat took place in the Nordic countries was a tiny, tiny war in northern Bohuslän. That same evening, the commanding officers brushed off their uniforms, curled their mustaches, and strode onto the squeaky floor of the inn at Kvistrum, and joined one another at the table. At least, that's the story which has been handed down throughout the province for more than two hundred years. And it's almost true.

In the autumn of 1788, Gustav III was staging a war against the Russian empress, in order to contain internal unrest that had been provoked by the spirit of revolt on the Continent. A year later, the French Revolution would break out. Denmark, the old enemy to the southwest, smelling revolution in the air, declared war on Sweden. With a Norwegian army, it would attack from the north, hoping to put an end to Swedish domination of Bohuslän. Leading the attack was Crown Prince Fredrik.

Second in command on the Dano-Norwegian side was Prince Carl of Hesse, brother-in-law of Gustav III. The army marched slowly southward through the chilly, damp countryside. Both princes and their staffs "dropped in" on the largest farms along the route. The soldiers had to bed down as best they could – in wet leaves, in empty barns or beneath overhanging trees.

The Swedes awaited them at Kvistrum, just north of today's Munkedal, at a site which had served that purpose well since the Middle Ages. But a Swedish lieutenant-colonel, Baron Ulric Funck, had stationed himself by the road a couple of miles farther north. When the Dano- Norwegian officers rode past, he bowed to them and made a request. Would the

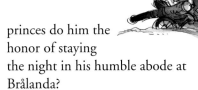

princes do him the honor of staying the night in his humble abode at Brålanda?

It must have been a bizarre scene. In the midst of a declared war, there was the enemy: the princes with their officers and escort, bone-weary, their horses covered in mud from the journey; and a Swedish officer, in fluent French, offering them his own military residence.

And, they accepted. They later continued south to the bridge at Kvistrum, and occupied the entire surrounding area. Finally, they returned to Brålanda for some more Swedish hospitality. No one seems to have considered that it might have been a strategic move, and in fact it wasn't.

Only a few weeks earlier, Baron Funck had cleared out his farm, in anticipation of war. He emptied his storehouses, packed up all food and furnishings and loaded everything onto wagons which were driven to safety behind Swedish lines. But now he ordered all the hay which had been strewn on the floors to protect them from dampness during his

absence, swept away. And he brought back all the wagons with their loads. The farm was cleaned up in a hurry and a huge spread was laid.

At this time of year, the farms were full of food. Animals had been slaughtered and vegetables, fruit and berries filled the pantries.

Mushrooms were not yet very popular, but were gaining approval, and there was plenty of grain in the grain in the storehouses after a hot summer.

As the illustrious guests entered the military residence at Brålanda, Prince Carl of Hesse made a proposal. It would please him greatly if the Swedish commander, Colonel Tranefelt, ate supper with them. Funck, the host, immediately sent an invitation. The colonel replied that, regrettably, he could not come that evening. But he promised to come the following day – for dinner!

After supper, the two princes and their officers went to bed under the enemy's roof. They probably slept well, and they took it easy in the morning. At midday, the Swedish colonel announced his arrival. He was ready to enjoy the princes' banquet.

There they sat, the Swedish and Danish commanding officers enjoying the hospitality of a Swedish military residence – in the midst of a Danish-Swedish war. They enjoyed the delights of the table well into the afternoon. At 2:30, the Swedish officers rose and heartily thanked their enemies and galloped off.

The war began that very day. There were two battles on successive days, each lasting 45 minutes. Each fired off some salvos for duty's sake – unfortunately at one another, so there were casualties: 11 dead and many wounded.

Yet, as wars go, losses were light, even if the families of the victims might disagree. It ended as politely as it began. The Swedes capitulated, but no one was taken prisoner. They were allowed to return home as long as they agreed not to fight any more. And the Dano-Norwegian army, which had marched so amicably into Bohuslän, retraced its steps home that November.

Pia Gadd

"The food lesson I'll never forget"

TECHNOLOGY HAD made its entrance into Skövde's gastronomic world. I had ordered pancakes at the local motel and paid. Now I was waiting for my food at the counter. "You don't need to wait here. We'll call out your food on the loudspeaker. It's a new system," explained the cashier.

At the table, I marvelled over technical progress that benefits mankind.

"One meatball! One omelet! One bacon and egg!" shrieked a voice from the big black box.

A few minutes later it was my turn, and the shout aroused giggles throughout the premises.

"One thin pancakes!"

As I look back on it with fond memories, I was on my way "home" to Skövde, to host a food festival in the early 1990s.

Food Festival in Skövde? It sounded strange. It was difficult to find any connection between the tiny town of Skövde in Skaraborg and gastronomic delights. The two seemed mutually exclusive.

Culinary and gastronomic excesses in my old home town were limited to the sensational advent of french fries at Oxen Restaurant in the 1960s and to poison-green marzipan covered cream cakes (popularly known as "vacuum cleaners") at Schmidt's school canteen.

But a food festival in Skaraborg...?

Maybe some creative, trendy cooks with insider knowledge of Nouvelle Cuisine could produce an exotic local dish or two – such as Braised Herons with Whitefish Caviar, topped with West Göta cheese.

There was one important issue, given the local residents' economic caution: How to deal with the relationship between first-class raw materials and price. I remember Runo Sandberg's classic remark at the meat counter, when he heard the price of sausages:

"Cut as close to the sausage as you can!"

Once I arrived in Skövde, all my doubts vanished. People came by the thousands – indeed, by the tens of thousands. They ate and drank, and the all the restaurateurs celebrated like lottery winners. It was simply "Folksy, Festive, and Fully Booked".

The "Grand Old Man" of Swedish cuisine, Tore Wretman, graced the festival with his presence. We spoke for a long time about his contributions to the development of the kitchen arts in Sweden. Towards the end of the interview, I changed the subject from food to drink.

"I've always heard you talk about food, but never about drink. Why don't you sing the praises of wine, as everyone else does?"

"I do, but softly," answered Wretman. "Because I don't consider myself a wine expert."

He continued:

"I can tell the difference between red and white, good and not so good. And I've managed well enough with that..."

Suddenly, I saw another familiar figure in the crowd, Kent from Moholm. A little rounder and a little balder than the last time, but the same guy, nonetheless.

We had been classmates, and despite all the years, I had not forgotten him – for a special reason. He gave me my first lesson in culinary theory.

There had been a showdown at school. Half the class came from Skövde, the other half from the countryside. Sometimes the conflicting sides lost control;

In this instance, one of the townies called a classmate a "stupid hick".

The teacher quickly took the matter in hand. His decided that the Skövdans needed to learn more about farm life and just how important farmers were for everyone.

"We should be proud of the Skaraborgan farmer. Every time you sit down at table, you should be grateful to him. Think of all the food on your table, the bread, butter, flour, milk, meat, and vegetables," urged the teacher.

As a conclusion, he said:

"Without our farmers, our lives would be poor."

Kent, the son of a dairy farmer, had to give a lecture about cows – but he was not very enthusiastic.

Week after week, the teacher reminded him about the lecture, but he always managed to find an excuse.

After two months, the teacher was fed up:

"Kent, you won't get off again. The time has come!"

Unwillingly, Kent dragged himself to the podium. He hadn't given a thought to the lecture, but he realized that he had to find something to say just to get it over with.

Rather embarrassed and clearly nervous, Kent cleared his throat and stated dryly:

"A cow...she has five udders...four for milk and one for cream!"

Then, with tangible relief, Kent shuffled back to his desk.

As I was leaving Skövde and the festival, I realized that I had been wrong. Reality had pulverized my narrow-minded prejudices about local interest in food. The food festival has flourished for many years and it is an important annual event in Skövde.

On my way to the car, I ran into a policeman on patrol.

"Say, I need to get to Stockholm in a hurry. Do you know if there are any speed controls on the way?" I said in my friendliest most flattering voice.

The policeman knotted his brow and replied gruffly:

"Belfrage, you've got to learn two things. Never fry bacon with your shirt off, and don't ever drive too fast outside Örebro."

Fredrik Belfrage

Hunting stories from Västra Götaland

I HAVE HUNTED MY ENTIRE LIFE. Already as a twelve-year-old, I went with my father to hunt hare and woodcock in Sörmland. Even then, I was fascinated by the atmosphere of the forest, the excitement during a resounding chase, the animals I got to see, and the fun I had with the others in Papa's hunting party. Since that time, I have gone through life with my camera and my shotgun. I have bagged a lot of game and even more memories over the years. I will never forget all the wonderful hunts in Västra Götaland, the many years of shooting grouse in Jämtland, and moose hunting in Västerbotten. I have shot more than 200 moose.

Västra Götaland is a wonderful county, Mother Nature at her best, with deep forests and high mountains, as well as great plains, pastures and meadows. We have both the sea coast and the inland sea of Vänern.

Our county is a great pantry, with fish from the ocean and lakes, meat from farms and hunting grounds, as well as berries and mushrooms from the forests.

Of course we are both proud and grateful for all the wonderful and delicious foodstuffs we have all around us.

MOOSE HUNTING IN WET SOCKS

I remember a moose hunt at Remningstorp, twelve miles east of Skara, where I lived for a while.

We had called a well-known dog-handler with an experienced Jämtland spitz, and there were many of us at the most important stations. Baying is beautiful! But it soon turned into walking – the moose moved at moderate speed with the dog barking after them, and they all headed north. Another short bay, and then total silence. The moose had probably bolted, followed by the dog.

Someone had caught a glimpse of a bull as it crossed the border. Before long, we heard baying, but it was far away on foreign soil.

It would take considerable time to retrieve the dog, which was accustomed to long drives in Norrland.

Everyone gathered to decide on a new strategy. Some hunters tried to track him down, while the rest of us waited around, with no result.

The day passed while we waited for the dog. The hunt ended, and we dispersed.

My car was half a mile away. Glad to be alone, I set out to look for tracks, I took a shortcut on a little forest road.

Suddenly I saw an young female crossing the road, 60–70 meters ahead. I tore off my boots, left them in the ditch, and loaded a cartridge into the chamber of my 30-06.

Now I had to be both quick and quiet. Half-running at first, I then sneaked cautiously into a small marsh, feeling the water between my toes. She was just 50 meters in front of me. She turned and presented a broadside. The shot was easy.

Just as I was about to approach and dress her, I saw a bull 100 meters farther away in the marsh. I sank slowly to my knees and sighted carefully. The bull fell at the shot. I went forward to inspect and dress it. Being alone made things a bit difficult, but I had a long cord and tied one rear leg up to a tree. The dressing proceeded nicely and I continued with the female.

With my shotgun over my back, and moose blood on my hands in spite of washing in the marsh-water, I padded out onto the road to the car in my soaking socks. Not wanting to get my boots wet inside, I carried them in one hand.

At last, I drove home to the farm and reported two shot moose for collection!

Long afterward, while eating a lovely stew made from the meat of my wet-socks moose, I couldn't help but laugh. I loved the looks on everyone's faces when I got home that time, and I was very proud!

GROUSE HUNTING WITH A FINNISH SPITZ

Forsvik Forest, on the edge of Tiveden, sounded exciting. I had arranged a meeting with Eric at Herrgården to hunt capercaillie, also known as wood grouse, with my Finnish spitz. That is my favorite kind of hunting and Eric was coming with me.

He had seen some cocks and even some black grouse on his grounds.

We went through fine woodlands, of both old and young stock. We went up and over rather high hills with the odd pine tree, and of course, we passed through the areas where Eric had seen the birds.

Nätti, my spitz, was on the look-out the whole time. She would stay out for 5–10 minutes before returning.

Suddenly we heard baying, 70–80 meters ahead of us. Down with the face-mask, on with the green gloves... I crept as carefully as I could toward the high fir tree where Nätti was barking. I studied every branch through my binoculars, but I didn't see a single bird – but they can be quite hard to see. Slowly I went to Nätti and followed her gaze upward. I couldn't see a thing. Eric made his way toward us.

Nätti kept barking up at the top of the fir.

We paced around the tree. It could hardly be a bird, though perhaps a marten or squirrel.

Finally I spotted something bushy and brown near the top: a squirrel's tail!

We just put Nätti on her leash and continued walking.

Another time, I was so certain that Nätti was barking persistently at a squirrel under an extremely tall, thin pine that I went to her and said, "Come, Nätti, let's go!"

But she wouldn't stop barking. I stood almost directly under the tree and scoured its top with my binoculars. Then I noticed a tiny, shiny black patch among the needles. I aimed and shot – and down fell a young cock of the wood!

This satisfied Nätti, and I was proud of her for not giving up. Besides, I was lucky not to have frightened away the cock when I called my little dog.

THE FOX'S LUNCH

It was –13°C (about 8°F). I sat out on the porch of Gösta's and my cabin. There's a cove of water between it and the main house, and there's a little road down from the heights behind the house toward the water.

The moon was nearly full, and the ground was white with snow and ice. Cold air bit my cheeks. I was waiting for a fox.

After almost three hours, I saw a shape

PhotoDisc: Nature, Wildlife and the Environment

coming fast down the road from the high hills. A fox – but it looked strange, and it had something big in its mouth... It was in a hurry. The distance was still too great. Soon it was straight in front of me, at 50–60 meters, and then it disappeared behind a large bush at the water's edge...

For a moment I could not decide whether to shoot. The fox trotted forward along the road again. My shot echoed in the cold night. The fox was down.

I strode down to the water, walked across the ice and went onto the road.

Next to the dead fox lay a big hind leg from a hare. Completely frozen.

By the following day, the hare leg had thawed, and Gösta and I roasted it for dinner.

For a long time the fox pelt hung in the cabin but eventually I put it away.

Getting rid of the fox was a good thing, since we raised birds. But not only did I take his life and his pelt – I also took his dinner.

HUNTING HAS ENRICHED MY LIFE
I have gotten a lot out of hunting.

It isn't every time one hunts that a shot can be pulled off and a quarry felled. But

each time, I experience nature intensely around me: small golden-crested wrens seeking food on a neighboring pine branch, a flock of long-tailed titmice moving past in the birch brush, the "wrong" animal going over the station, a moose during a deer hunt, a fox when stalking moose…

In purely physical terms, hunting has certainly added to my strength, endurance and patience.

I enjoy the friendship of my hunting partners, and I have made many friends through hunting.

Last but not least comes the cooperation with a clever, beloved dog. Being out in the forest hunting birds with my Finnish spitz, Nätti – that's what happiness means to me!

Astrid Bergman Sucksdorff

Astrid's game recipes

MOOSE AND ROE DEER FILET

I usually remove the long, fine strip loins on a roe deer saddle while I am butchering the hanging animal. I prepare both moose and roe deer filet in the same way.

I rub the meat with salt and white pepper, and on moose, garlic powder. Then, I brown the meat on all sides in a hot, cast iron pan. Then, I add a little water, cover, and lower the heat. After about 10 minutes, a roe deer filet is done. Moose takes a few minutes longer. Be careful not to overcook the meat. Check with a skewer to see if the meat juices are rosy. Both filets have to rest for a while before slicing.

The meat should be bright pink within an edge of dark brown.

It is often so good and tender that it melts in the mouth.

There's no need for sauce. Natural juices are good, preferably a combination of natural juices and crème fraiche (maybe even a little cream), white and black pepper, a little soy sauce, crushed juniper berries and currant jelly.

ROAST SADDLE OF HARE

with Brussels sprouts, potatoes, rowanberry jelly and a good cream sauce with crushed juniper berries, salt, pepper and a little soy

sauce is delicious. The saddle should be a beautiful brown and the meat slightly pink. Brown, then roast, covered, on top of the stove, from 10 to 30 minutes, depending upon size.

The legs make a good stew. Cut into pieces and season with salt and pepper. Brown, then transfer to a saucepan just large enough. Add wine and bring to a boil. Then brown large onion wedges. When the meat is about half cooked, add the onions (otherwise the onions will turn to mush). Cook the meat until tender.

ROE DEER AND MOOSE CALVES LIVER

are much better than many think. I make both kinds the same way. Finely browned and lightly sautéed slices are good served with either cream sauce, rice and lingonberry compote, or the way I like best, with fried onions and potatoes, preferably mashed.

In both cases, it is important to brown the slices well, then season with salt and white pepper. They should be a little pink inside. As they are ready, I transfer them to a serving platter.

Overcooked liver is like shoe leather and

does not belong on any table.

Begin by frying the onion until soft. A little sugar gives it both color and aroma. Slices of liver cook quickly in a frying pan, and they should be eaten immediately. That's when they are best.

ROAST BONELESS MOOSE
weighing about 1 kilo (2 1/4 lb) from the round or sirloin will be fine if you prepare it this way:

Rub the meat with salt and black pepper and place in an ovenproof dish. Insert a meat thermometer into the thickest part. Roast at 125°C (260°F) until the meat reaches an internal temperature of 63°C (145°F). Transfer to a cutting board.

Wrap in aluminum foil and let the meat rest at least 10 minutes before slicing.

The secret of this roast meat is the low oven temperature – don't be tempted to increase the heat to 175°C (350°F) or even 150°C (300°F). The roast takes time, almost two hours, so plan accordingly.

The result is always good: pink all the way through.

For almost well-done meat, roast the meat until the meat reaches an internal temperature of 70°C (158°F).

YOUNG WOOD GROUSE
Doesn't take longer to cook than potatoes. Cut out both breasts of a young grouse. Rub them with salt and white pepper and brown in a frying pan. Lower heat and cover, preferably with a glass lid (always interesting to watch).

After 12-16 minutes, they are ready. Check by inserting a skewer. Cover with foil and let rest.

Deglaze the pan with cream, more pepper and a little soy sauce and black currant jelly. Just before serving, add a dash of sherry or port wine.

The potatoes are ready, and more jelly is in a bowl. I like a crispy endive salad alongside. Decant a bottle of full-bodied red wine and serve with the meat.

Light the candles and cut the breasts into even slices. The feeling of satisfaction is spreading through the air.

The great joy of catching mackerel

WE BOARDED THE BOAT AND set out to sea in the afternoon. The mackerel net filled the entire boat – there was hardly room to move. Other fishermen, professionals, who started at the same time had passed us by much earlier. Now the wind slackened too; I reefed and started our auxiliary motor. It seemed slower than ever. When darkness began to fall, Håkan looked at his watch.

"We can't go out any farther or we won't get back in time to load the truck to take the fish to auction."

For better or worse, we let out the net. Fishing for mackerel means that the boat pulls the float-chains slowly, keeping them stretched in order to catch anything.

At midnight, a huge school suddenly swam into the chain and all the shimmering bodies were trapped tightly within the net.

We pulled the chain on board – it was an incredible catch. First we filled the pantry, but that was only the beginning. Once all the linkage was raised, I slid like a seal across the catch and back out on deck, or more exactly to a bench on the side. We were loaded to the railings. The five boxes we had

brought along for our catch were absurdly inadequate.

Håkan was rapturous. These wonderful fresh mackerel! What pleasure they would bring to many a table in Gothenburg in a few hours! He described how we would prepare our own fish once we got home. We would follow Bengt Petersen's superb recipe, coeur de filet provençale smothered in ovenbaked diced potatoes, but with fresh mackerel instead of meat. What a delicacy!

Meanwhile, one fishing boat after another bustled past us, on the way back to the harbor where the truck waited. We saw how efficiently they worked on their spacious decks, freeing the net from the mackerel. We had long since filled our boxes and were tangled in net up to our waists. The cabin floor was carpeted with mackerel.

This gigantic cargo slowed Fidran down. Once we reached the harbor entrance, we met the pros on their way home, and we didn't really like the look of their broad smiles. Quite right: as we reached the harbor, we saw the truck pulling out onto the road to Gothenburg.

There was nothing we could do, but we had to find someone to take the catch.

I called a fishmonger in Kungälv. No, thanks – he had already been promised big catches of mackerel.

A man approached us as we had laid to. He stood with his hands in his pockets and looked down at us in Fidran.

"And where did you get that chain?" he asked, as if he suspected we'd stolen it. Then he looked toward the east. "The sun will soon be hot," he added. "Not good for the mackerel."

He disappeared, whistling, into the store-house.

We recognized him – he owned a busy fish market. Now we hurried to buy more boxes and plucked the mackerel out of the net as fast as we could. Hungry gulls sat in a row along the cliff edge and waited in vain for breakfast. Mackerel isn't gutted, and that's why it has to be very fresh.

Quality is measured by the resistance of the flesh when grasped at the neck, as teachers used to do with mischievous pupils. If the fish is a little soft and the fingers sink in a few millimeters, it's too late: the mackerel tastes like cod liver oil. Anyone who has ever eaten such a fish deems it inedible and never wants to try it again.

We toiled and stressed as the merciless sun climbed, ever hotter. Now and then, the fishmonger emerged. He looked at our full boxes and pinched a few necks. He muttered that they didn't look like much to him. And again he disappeared into the building.

When we finally were finished, the air was lukewarm. The fishmonger stood there once more. We looked up at him, as though kneeling before a priest: would he save us?

"I'll take care of them to help you," he said at last. "So you won't have to drive it all away to Ängholmen. But I can't give you more for them than they would have paid over there."

Ängholmen's factory grinds down rotten fish and scraps to make chicken-feed and fertilizer.

That was that. As soon as we settled the deal, a truck rolled up and swiftly took our catch into cold storage. We were paid for one ton, a ton of scraps.

Later, we learned what had happened to the fish that reached the auction in time. Not a single kilo was sold to the people of Gothenburg. Outside the entrance were a couple of trucks that had driven down from Norway, where the school of mackerel had arrived a little earlier. The Norwegians offered their cargo to the fishmongers who were actually going in to the auction. Their mackerel had been caught the previous day, and the buyers got it for rock-bottom prices.

So the Swedish mackerel caught only hours earlier couldn't be sold – it went to scrap.

Luckily, we earned a few more cents for our catch. That consoled us as we enjoyed our magnificent, fragrant coeur de maquereau provençale and a bottle of German Hochheimer Stielweg, a Riesling Spätlese. Since events took place when the French were testing atom bombs in the Pacific, we boycotted their wines. Otherwise, we would have chosen a Chablis Grand Cru, without a doubt.

Birgitta Stenberg

Fried mackerel with garlic

FOUR SERVINGS
8 mackerel fillets
salt
butter
fried potatoe

Garlic butter:
100 g (3 1/2 oz) unsalted butter
2-3 garlic cloves, crushed
1 tablespoon chopped parsley
a few drops lemon juice
pinch salt

Sprinkle fillets with salt and fry in butter until golden brown. While the fish is frying, combine butter, garlic, parsley, lemon juice and salt. Preheat the grill. Arrange the fried potatoes on an ovenproof serving dish. Top with fish and spread with garlic butter. Place under the grill until the butter has melted over the fish and potatoes. Serve immediately.

Bengt Petersen

Tall tales with coffee

I LOVE FOOD. That you should not order whiskey with goose liver does not mean that you can't order them separately. I really love food. But if you're going to waste anything in life, it shouldn't be time. I walk fast, so I don't have time to be in the kitchen very often.

I've been married to Monika for many years. Her father, Börje Persson, was restaurateur at Svaneholm Castle in Skåne. He loved big parties. At a duck dinner once,

I asked – loudly so everyone could hear – for ketchup. I understood from their reaction that my wish was not considered proper at the moment...

Börje Persson was principally against drinking whiskey before 4 p.m. But several times I saw him setting his watch ahead an hour. What some people won't do to enjoy that – ah, so excellent – drink!

I once spent three days in the Champagne district of France trampling grapes for champagne. Since then, it tastes better; maybe my feet contributed to the contents of the bottle I happen to be enjoying with my friends.

However, I have also had the opportunity to sample unusual dishes. During a visit to Mongolia's capital, Ulan-Bator, I was offered a breakfast of cold horse-tongue with Coca-Cola or Pepsi. At lunch, I could order the same well-composed menu again.

I declined both times.

But at dinner, a different combination was served: hot horse-tongue with Coca-Cola or Pepsi. I jumped at the chance – it was a taste sensation I'll always remember. And I must admit that my own tongue was quicker than usual that evening.

In Tonga, I was invited to dine with south sea Vikings – as the inhabitants of this island are known. The King of Tonga was also present. We were offered fish, mussels, and root vegetables in palm leaves that had been baked in a fire pit covered with stones.

The King of Tonga once weighed 260 kilos (572 lb), but he had slimmed down to 170 kilos (375 lb). I tried to reciprocate the hospitality by offering His Majesty some shaved reindeer meat I had brought along.

"No, thanks," said the King, giving a simple explanation: "I didn't bring my false teeth." Such frankness must be unusual in royal circles elsewhere.

I once made a gastronomic tour with a lovely woman. Ordering Biff à la Greta, I asked for French fries in stead of the potatoes served with the dish. How was I to know that this flatly contradicted the dish's correct composition? Without potatoes, there can be no Biff à la Greta.

I love Swedish country cooking – pea soup, finely and coarsely ground sausages, mashed turnips...hmmm. With good raw materials, these dishes are unique culinary experiences.

Yet if anyone wants to treat me to an ideal menu, I prefer the following:
– snails in garlic (Provençale)
– a big minute steak with parsley butter and potatoes au gratin
– deep-fried camembert, cloudberry preserves or parsley.

With this, I like a beer or water, and coffee with cognac.

An additional specialty, which I have adored since childhood, is hollowed-out bark bread with peanut filling. I hollow out the bread myself, and keep the "shell". Then I fill it with peanuts and eat it with pleasure. I have not found this in any cookbook...

Good stories are also part of a good meal. A hearty laugh whets the appetite and enhances a meal. I prefer anecdotes from Gothenburg.

Such as this one:

Karl and Osborn meet, and Karl asks:

"*Have you heard that Evert has become impotent?*"

"*Good grief,*" answers Osborn, "*he never even finished elementary school.*"

Ingvar Oldsberg

* GOOD GRIEF....

Alängen's hearty mushroom soup

FOUR SERVINGS
*150 g (5 oz) sliced
bacon
1 onion
2 medium carrots
1 liter (4 cups) fresh
funnel chanterelles or
regular chanterelles
4 dl (1 2/3 cups)
shredded leek
6 dl (2 1/2 cups) full
fat milk
2 dl (3/4 cup)
whipping cream
1/2 teaspoon soy sauce
2 vegetable bouillon
cubes
1 1/2 teaspoons thyme
1/4 teaspoon salt
freshly ground
white pepper*

Mushroom soup can be rather tasteless. In this recipe, the flavor is enhanced with bacon and carrots to make a hearty dish, which can be served as a main course. With sandwiches and dessert, it makes a filling meal. If serving as an appetizer, decrease milk and increase cream for a more full-bodied soup.

PREPARATION TIME: *30-40 minutes*
Cut bacon into shreds. Chop onion and shred carrots. Clean and coarsely chop mushrooms. Fry without added fat until any liquid has evaporated and about 3 dl (1 1/4 cups) mushrooms remain. Fry bacon in its own fat until crisp. Dry on paper towels. Sauté onion and leek.
Transfer all ingredients to a large saucepan and simmer over low heat until carrots are tender. Season with salt and pepper.

BEVERAGE SUGGESTION: A beverage is not always necessary with soup, but a white Chardonnay wine, with a few years behind it, is excellent with this dish.

Björn Lingehed, Tibro

Potato-leek cappuccino

FOUR SERVINGS
*2 medium potatoes
(of a mealy variety)
1/2 onion
1/2 garlic clove
1 medium leek
1/4 teaspoon thyme
1 bay leaf
2 tablespoons butter
3 dl (1 1/4 cups)
water
3 dl (1 1/4 cups)
coffee cream
or half and half
1 chicken bouillon
cube*

This creamy soup uses a regional product as its base. For an elegant touch, garnish with shellfish or golden caviar.

PREPARATION TIME: *30 minutes*
SERVING SUGGESTION: *Garnish with crayfish or shrimp.*

Peel and cut potatoes into 1/2 cm (1/4") slices.
Peel and slice onion. Mince garlic. Slice 10 cm (4") of leek, then shred the rest.
Sauté vegetables and seasonings in butter over low heat about 4 minutes.
Add water and cream and crumble in bouillon cube. Simmer until vegetables are tender. Pour into a food processor and puree until smooth.

BEVERAGE SUGGESTION: A white wine, dry or semi-dry, goes well with this soup. If the soup is garnished with shellfish, a Muscadet is especially good.

Ulrik Lindelöv, Alingsås

ALÄNGEN'S HEARTY MUSHROOM SOUP

Fine fish crèpes

SIX SERVINGS
12 crèpes:
2 dl (3/4 cup) flour
5 dl (2 cups) milk
3 eggs
2 tablespoons melted butter

Filling:
1 small onion
butter
500 g (1 1/4 lb) white fish
fillets, such as cod or
haddock
2 dl (3/4 cup) crème
fraiche or whipping cream
salt and pepper
2 tablespoons chopped dill
125 g (4 oz) tin or
jar mussels
2 dl (3/4cup) grated
Gruyere or Swiss cheese

Sauce:
2 1/2 (1 cup) dairy
sour cream
3/4 dl (1/3 cup) chili sauce
(ketchup-style)
salt and pepper
sliced olives

Crepes were the height of sophistication during the 1970s. They were served both as an appetizer and as a light meal. Today's version is often served as a pouch tied with a strip of blanched leek.

PREPARATION TIME: *40 minutes*
OVEN TEMPERATURE: *250°C (450°F)*

Whisk ingredients for crèpes in a blender until smooth. Let batter rest at least 30 minutes before preparing crèpes. Fry crepes over low heat and only on one side for best results. They can be prepared well in advance.
Chop onion and sauté in butter until soft. Cut fish into small chunks and add with crème fraiche. Season with salt and pepper. Add dill and simmer 3-5 minutes. Fold in mussels.
Divide filling among pancakes and roll up.
Place closely together in an ovenproof dish. Sprinkle with grated cheese. Bake about 15 minutes.
Combine all ingredients for sauce and serve cold with hot crèpes. Garnish with sliced olives.

Angélica Serrano-Punell, Hisings Backa

Eggs stuffed with mussel mousse

FOUR SERVINGS
4 eggs
1 tin (3-4 oz) smoked
mussels in oil
100 g (3 oz) cream cheese
1/2 teaspoon Dijon-style
mustard
1/2 teaspoon soy sauce
1 teaspoon lemon juice
salt and pepper
4 lettuce leaves
3-4 tablespoons chopped
chives

This quick and easy dish is equally good on a smörgås-bord. Slice eggs and arrange on slices of whole-grain bread, then top with mousse.

PREPARATION TIME: *About 20 minutes*

Cook eggs about 8 minutes, then plunge into cold water. Peel.
Drain excess oil from mussels and puree in a food processor with cheese, mustard, soy sauce and lemon juice until smooth. Season with salt and pepper.
Halve eggs lengthwise and place on a bed of lettuce. Dot eggs with mussel mousse and sprinkle with chives.

BEVERAGE SUGGESTION: This summer dish goes well with a cold beer, preferably one with a slightly bitter character.

Micke Danielsson, Gothenburg

Salt herring in egg sauce

FOUR SERVINGS
2 salt herrings
2 eggs
1 tablespoon mustard
(do not use hotdog mustard)
1/4 teaspoon salt
1/8 teaspoon white pepper
1 tablespoon sugar
1 tablespoon red wine vinegar
2 dl (3/4 cup) dairy sour cream
3 tablespoons chopped dill

This recipe is simple and easy to prepare. Ingredients have been chosen with western Swedish traditions in mind, and they are inexpensive as well. The herring are prepared according to turn-of-the-century taste, soaked overnight and still quite salty. In some places, it is possible to buy presoaked fillets, which makes this recipe even easier.

PREPARATION TIME: *30 minutes, in addition to soaking overnight or longer, plus at least one hour in the refrigerator before serving.*
SERVING SUGGESTION: *Serve with boiled potatoes, preferably new potatoes, and a salad.*

Clean herring and soak in 3-4 liters (quarts) of water overnight. Cut out fillets by pressing against the backbone with a knife on each side, then remove as many small bones as possible. Remove skin and cut fillets into 2 cm (1") wide lengths. Place on a serving platter.
Cook eggs about 8 minutes, then plunge into cold water. Peel. Slice lengthwise and scoop out yolks. Mash yolks with mustard, salt, pepper, sugar and vinegar. Stir in sour cream and dill, then pour over herring. Chop egg whites and sprinkle on top. Garnish with dill. Refrigerate at least one hour before serving.

Georg Hergert, Mariestad

Grilled juniper cheese salad

FOUR SERVINGS
1 head lettuce
3-4 small tomatoes
1 small red onion
black olives
1 egg, lightly beaten
1 1/2 dl (2/3 cup) dry breadcrumbs
4 slices juniper cheese, about 40 g (1 1/2 oz) each (or Swiss cheese with 4 crushed juniper berries sprinkled on top)

A green salad topped with grilled cheese is a favorite Mediterranean dish, and this is a Swedish variation. When composing the rest of the menu, take into consideration that cheese is very filling.

PREPARATION TIME: *20 minutes*

Rinse lettuce and tear into bite-size pieces. Thinly slice tomatoes and onion. Arrange lettuce on four plates. Top with tomato and onion slices. Garnish with olives.
Preheat grill. Dip cheese slices in beaten egg, then in crumbs. Place on aluminum foil, but do not wrap. Grill until golden. The breading should not fall off.
Place foil packet alongside the salad and serve immediately.

BEVERAGE SUGGESTION: A light red wine, served lightly chilled, or a well-chilled rosé are both good with this cheese course.

Margareta Bengtsson and Anna Rehnstedt, Falköping

SALT HERRING IN EGG SAUCE

Gratinéed shellfish

FOUR SERVINGS
300 g (10 oz) cooked shrimp
in the shell
4 medium ocean crayfish, cooked
1 cooked crab

Sauce:
1 tablespoon minced shallot
1 dl (1/2 cup) fish stock
1 dl (1/2 cup) dry white wine
1 1/2 dl (2/3 cup) whipping cream
2 tablespoons butter
salt and pepper
lemon juice
2 tablespoons grated Swiss cheese

Only the best is good enough in this dish of fresh, newly cooked shellfish in a delicate sauce.

PREPARATION TIME: *30 minutes*
OVEN TEMPERATURE: *275°C (425°F)*
SERVING SUGGESTION: *Serve with toast to mop up the sauce.*

Peel shrimp, then halve crayfish and crab lengthwise. Remove meat and cut into small pieces.
Simmer shallot and fish stock several minutes. Add white wine and cream and reduce over high heat until about half the original amount remains. Beat in butter and season with salt, pepper and lemon juice.
Arrange shellfish in individual ovenproof dishes. Spoon over sauce and sprinkle with cheese. Grill about 5-6 minutes, until cheese has melted and turned golden brown.

Micke Danielsson, Gothenburg

Onion tart

EIGHT SLICES
1 pie shell
400 g (14 oz) onions
butter
1 teaspoon dried thyme
1 teaspoon salt
1/4 teaspoon black pepper
2 dl (1 cup) grated Swiss cheese
2 dl (1 cup) whipping cream
black olives

Hot or cold, picnic or canapé, this onion tart is perfect, any time, any place. It is also good with a mixture of leeks, garlic and onion.

PREPARATION TIME: *80 minutes*
OVEN TEMPERATURE: *250°C (425°F) for pie shell,*
175°C (350°F) for pie

Prick pie shell all over with a fork and bake 10 minutes. Lower temperature.
Thinly slice onion and cook over low heat until soft. Season with thyme, salt and pepper. Arrange in the pre-baked pie shell.
Whisk eggs and cream together and pour over cheese. Bake about 30 minutes.
Garnish with black olives.

BEVERAGE SUGGESTION: Onion and wine are great friends. A chilled, fresh rosé is especially good with this thyme-flavored onion tart.

Sven Bartilsson, Tollered

GRATINÉED SHELLFISH

Fried perch fillets with chanterelles and spinach salad

FOUR SERVINGS
5 dl (2 cups) small chanterelles
1 tablespoon minced onion
2 tablespoons butter
200 g (8 oz) fresh spinach
1 tablespoon rapeseed oil
1/2 tablespoon white
wine vinegar
salt and pepper
about 400 g (14 oz) skinless
and boneless perch fillets
1/2 dl (3 1/2 tablespoons) flour
1 teaspoon salt
1/8 teaspoon pepper

There are those who just do not appreciate large catches of perch. The easiest way to deal with this fish is to gut and rinse it well, then bake at 200 °C (400 °F) for 20-30 minutes. Cool slightly, then remove skin and bones. It is delicious in salad, soup and other dishes. This recipe, however, uses raw perch fillets.

PREPARATION TIME: *30 minutes*
SERVING SUGGESTION: *Garnish with lemon wedges and parsley.*

Clean mushrooms and sauté with onion in butter until all liquid has evaporated and they begin to sizzle.
Rinse spinach, removing any large stalks.
Dry, then shred. Whisk oil, vinegar, and spices and pour over spinach. Toss, then arrange on four individual plates.
Dip fillets in flour seasoned with salt and pepper. Fry in butter until golden, about 2 minutes per side. Arrange fish on spinach with chanterelles all around.

Karen Pilgaard, Tibro

Bladder wrack salad

SIX SERVINGS
250 g (8 oz) bladder wrack

Marinade:
1 1/4 dl (1/2 cup) rapeseed oil
2 teaspoons lemon juice
2 tablespoons minced red onion
1/4 teaspoon dried basil
1/4 teaspoon dried thyme

Stronger version of marinade:
1 dl (1/3 cup) canned crushed tomatoes
1 1/4 teaspoons soy sauce
4-5 tablespoons chopped dill

Bladder wrack is often used to garnish seafood dishes. Try eating it this time! It has a fresh salty flavor and an interesting, chewy texture. It is important to use fresh seaweed.

PREPARATION TIME: *About 60 minutes plus marinating overnight*

Rinse bladder wrack well and cook in lightly salted water (1 tablespoon salt/liter (quart)) about 35 minutes. Combine all ingredients in marinade.
Layer seaweed and dill in a glass jar.
Pour over marinade and refrigerate overnight.
Serve as an appetizer or as a vegetable with fish and meat.

Göran Michanek, Gothenburg

FRIED PERCH FILLETS WITH CHANTERELLES AND SPINACH SALAD

Apple-corn chowder

FOUR SERVINGS
1 small onion
1 small sour apple
1 tablespoon butter
1 vegetable bouillon cube
500 g (1 1/4 lb) corn (frozen or canned)
1/2 teaspoon salt
1/4 teaspoon white pepper
1 dl (1/3 cup) whipping cream
2 tablespoons chopped parsley

Adding a sour apple is a good way to infuse an otherwise rather neutral dish with flavor.

PREPARATION TIME: *30 minutes*
SERVING SUGGESTION: *Serve with toasted white bread.*

Coarsely chop onion and apple and sauté in butter in a large saucepan until soft.
Add 8 dl (3 1/3 cups) water and bouillon cube. Heat until cube has dissolved. Reserve 1/2 dl (3 1/2 tablespoons) corn for garnish. Add remaining corn and bring to a boil. Season with salt and pepper and simmer 7-8 minutes.
Pour into a food processor and puree until smooth. Strain. Return soup to saucepan, add cream, and simmer 3-4 minutes. Season to taste.
Garnish with corn and parsley. Serve piping hot.

Bernt Wernlund, Kinna

Chicken liver mousse

FOUR SERVINGS
200 g (8 oz) chicken livers
150 g (5 oz) unsalted butter
1/2 teaspoon salt
1/4 teaspoon white pepper
2 tablespoons port wine
2 tablespoons cognac

This mousse is easy to make in larger quantities. Just remember that liver is highly perishable. Work quickly and store in the refrigerator.

PREPARATION TIME: *20 minutes plus two hours in the refrigerator*
SERVING SUGGESTION: *Serve with toast triangles, port wine jelly and lettuce leaves.*

Clean livers, removing any green spots and veins. Sauté in 2 tablespoons of the butter. The livers should be pink inside. Season with salt and pepper. Remove pan from heat, then add port wine and cognac. Cool.
Transfer to a food processor and puree until smooth.
With the motor running, add cold butter and puree until sooth. Refrigerate at least two hours.
Form small eggs of liver mousse with a spoon dipped in hot water.

BEVERAGE SUGGESTION: A spiced Alsace wine, preferably made with Pinot Gris grapes, goes very well with this flavorful chicken mousse.

Gunvor Fröberg, Anten

APPLE-CORN CHOWDER

Orange and herb-baked breast of wild duck with apple-lingonberry chutney

FOUR SERVINGS
Chutney:
1 red onion
2 sour apples
rind and juice of 1 lemon
1/2 teaspoon ground cloves
1/4 teaspoon ground cinnamon
1/4 teaspoon ground cardamom
1 tablespoon corn oil
2 tablespoons raspberry vinegar
1/2 teaspoon salt
1 tablespoon dark brown sugar
1 dl (1/2 cup) lingonberries
1 1/2 tablespoons honey
2 wild duck breasts

Stuffing:
rind and juice of 1/2 orange
1 teaspoon sugar
1/2 teaspoon salt
1/2 teaspoon white pepper
1 dl (1/2 cup) chopped fresh herbs, such as basil, parsley, coriander

Wild duck, pheasant and even chicken can be used in this dish. Chutney is inexpensive and easy to make, and the blend of spices can be varied as desired. Try using pear, mango or peach instead of apple.

PREPARATION TIME: *Chutney about 30 minutes plus three days in the refrigerator to mature; duck about 40 minutes.*

CHUTNEY:
Shred onion, apples and lemon rind. Carefully sauté with spices in oil.
Add lemon juice, vinegar, salt, sugar, lingonberries and honey. Simmer about 10 minutes, until apples begin to soften.
Pour into clean jars, then seal and refrigerate at least three days before serving.

DUCK:
Halve breasts horizontally and open to make a 15 cm (6") square. Place on plastic wrap. Combine stuffing ingredients and spread over meat.
Roll up as tightly as possible. Bind or tie. Place in a sauté pan with enough water to cover slightly. Cover and simmer over low heat (85°C, 185°F) 15 minutes.
Slice roulade and serve, lukewarm or cold, on a bed of salad greens. Spoon chutney alongside.

BEVERAGE SUGGESTION: In this dish, the full-bodied flavor of wild duck is combined with the sweet and sour orange. A red Burgundy is the classic choice – a more budget-friendly alternative is a wine made with Pinot Noir grapes from other parts of the world, or one made with Merlot grapes.

Janne Hedman, Lundsbrunn

Baked beets

FOUR SERVINGS
500 g (1 1/4 lb) fresh beets (7-8 small)

Anchovy butter:
6 Swedish-style anchovy fillets
2 tablespoons chopped leek
75 g (5 tablespoons) unsalted butter, softened

The intense color and flavor of the beets are a good contrast with vivid yellow anchovy butter. Serve with whole grain bread. Remember that beets contain nitrates and should not be given to children less than one year old.

PREPARATION TIME: *About 50 minutes*
OVEN TEMPERATURE: *225°C (425°F)*

Wash beets. Bake on an oven rack about 40 minutes. Reduce cooking time for early beets.

ANCHOVY BUTTER:
Mince anchovies. Combine with leek and butter.
Serve with the warm beets.

BEVERAGE SUGGESTION: : A light beer with moderate bitterness is best with these beets with anchovy butter.

Ulrika Fröberg, Tollered

ORANGE AND HERB-BAKED BREAST OF WILD DUCK WITH APPLE-LINGONBERRY CHUTNEY

Salmon-filled pasta pillows with creamy crayfish sauce

FOUR SERVINGS

Pasta:
300 g (2 1/3 cups) durum
wheat flour
5 eggs
1 teaspoon salt
1 tablespoon olive oil

Sauce:
4 medium ocean crayfish or
8 freshwater crayfish
3 tablespoons corn oil
1 onion
1 medium carrot
75-100 g (3 oz) chunk celeriac
1 garlic clove
1 teaspoon powdered paprika
1 tablespoon dill seeds
1 tablespoon tomato paste
8 dl (3 1/3 cups) fish stock
2 dl (3/4 cup) white wine
3 dl (1 1/4 cups)
whipping cream
1 teaspoon cornstarch stirred into
1 tablespoon water (optional)

Filling:
200 g (7 oz) boneless and
skinless salmon fillet
1/2 teaspoon salt
1 egg white
1/2 dl (3 1/2 tablespoons)
whipping cream

Cheese chips:
40 g (1 1/2 oz) cheddar cheese

This festive pasta dish is a long way from the macaroni dishes of the 1950s. Either kind of crayfish works well in this dish.

PREPARATION TIME: *1 1/2 hours plus 1 hour resting time.*
SERVING SUGGESTION: *Place pillows on heated plates. Spoon over hot sauce. Garnish with crayfish tails and cheese chips.*

Arrange flour in a mound. Lightly beat eggs. Make a cavity in the center and add remaining ingredients. Knead until smooth and elastic (10-15 minutes). This pasta also can be made in a food processor. Cover and let rest about one hour. Divide into two equal parts. Roll each into thin sheets.
Peel crayfish, reserving meat for decoration. Preheat oven to 125°C (250°F) Dry shells in oven for about one hour. Crush. In a large saucepan, sauté crushed shells in oil a few minutes. Be careful not to let shells burn or stock will be bitter.
Shred vegetables and mince garlic. Add to pan and sauté a few minutes more. Add seasonings and tomato puree.
Stir in stock and wine. Bring slowly to a boil, then simmer 20 minutes.
Strain, then return to pan and reduce over medium heat until half the original amount remains. Add cream and reduce once more. Season with salt. If sauce is too thin, thicken with cornstarch mixture.

PASTA PILLOWS:
Cut fish into small pieces and place in a food processor with salt. With motor running, add egg white and cream. Do not overprocess or mixture will get hot and cream will leach out. Refrigerate salmon mixture.
In a large saucepan, bring water to a boil. Add oil and salt. Place pasta dough on a flat surface. Dot or pipe salmon mousse in small mounds on the pasta. Count on 3-4 per person. Brush around each mound of mousse with warm water, so that top sheet of dough will stick to bottom sheet.
Press out "pillows" with a cookie cutter or glass. Add pillows carefully to boiling water. Cook 2-3 minutes. They float to the top when ready.
Place pillows on heated plates, then spoon over hot sauce.

CHEESE CHIPS:
Preheat oven to 175°C (350°F). Divide cheese into four pieces of equal size.
Place far apart on a cookie sheet lined with parchment paper. Melt in oven about 7-8 minutes, until they have spread out and turned golden brown.

Lagman's Gymnasium, Vara

Lobster fishing – a passionate industry

IF MOOSE HUNTING is every Norrlander's dream all summer, then the first day of lobster season is the high point of the year along the coast of Bohuslän. Lobsters are a delicacy, the undisputed rulers of the deep and prize catch along the coast. Especially the females. Everyone agrees they're best.

As early as the 1600s, lobsters were caught in Bohuslän. During the centuries that followed, they were shipped live to England and sent by stagecoach to Stockholm.

Even today, lobster fishing is a passionate industry, and a good lobster fisherman deserves his high status. Knowledge of the best spots and favorite hiding places, as well as trapping techniques, are often passed from father to son. And there's no mercy for anyone caught breaking the rules or trapping before the season officially begins.

Lobster poaching is a sensitive topic: "Steal a couple of lobsters and you're marked for life".say those who know.

Lobster season begins at the stroke of 7:00 am on the first Monday after September 20. But hours before that time, enthusiastic lobster fishermen gather in the morning mist, like expectant fans at a rock concert. Side by side, amateur and professional fishermen guide their boats, laden with lobster pots, traps and nets, through the darkness to the best spots. It's important to be in the right place when the foghorn sounds and the lobster is fair game once again.

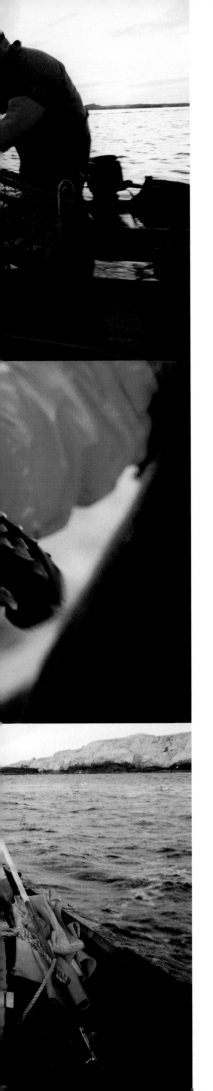

Boiled lobster

Lobster, about 400 g (14 oz) each

6 liters (quarts) water
about 100 g (1/3 cup) salt
about 5 dl (2 cups) dark beer

Rinse lobster in running water. Bring water and salt to a boil, then add beer. Water should be boiling when lobster is added.
Simmer lobster 8-10 minutes, until temperature where head joins tail reaches 69°C (155°F). Measure with an instant-read thermometer. Chill as quickly as possible. Chill the cooking liquid and keep refrigerated.

The Lobster Academy, Hunnebostrand

Lobster soup

FOUR SERVINGS
shells from 4 lobsters
1 onion
1 carrot
1 parsnip
2-3 tablespoons tomato paste
3 dl (1 1/4 cups) whipping cream
2 1/2 tablespoons cognac
salt and white pepper

Preheat oven to 200°C (400°F). Crush lobster shells. Cube root vegetables.
Place shells and vegetables on an oven tray and bake 20 minutes. Transfer to a large saucepan. Add water to cover, then simmer 30 minutes. Strain broth into a new saucepan, discarding shells and vegetables. Add cream and reduce until about 1 liter (quart) remains. Just before serving, add cognac, salt and pepper.

The Lobster Academy, Hunnebostrand

Salmon-stuffed cabbage rolls with saffron sauce

FOUR SERVINGS
Salmon filling:
3 g (1/10 oz) dried cepes
15 g (1/2 oz) dried funnel chanterelles
500 g (1 1/4 lb) skinless and boneless salmon fillet
50 g (2 oz) smoked salmon
2 tablespoons chopped chives
1 dl (1/2 cup) whipping cream
1 teaspoon salt
1/4 teaspoon white pepper
1 head cabbage

Fish stock:
1 dl (1/2 cup) white wine
6 dl (2 1/2 cups) water
3 tablespoons concentrated fish stock (from a jar)
1/2 teaspoon salt

Saffron sauce:
4 dl (1 2/3 cups) cooking liquid from cabbage rolls
1 dl (1/2 cup) whipping cream
1/2 g (pinch) saffron
2 teaspoons cornstarch stirred into 1 tablespoon cold water (optional)

Root vegetable mix:
2 dl (3/4 cup) shredded carrot
2 dl (3/4 cup) shredded parsnip
2 dl (3/4 cup) shredded celeriac
2 tablespoons butter
1 teaspoon salt
2 tablespoons chopped parsley

This is a festive dish made with salmon from Vänern. It requires a number of steps to make, but it is worth the effort.

PREPARATION TIME: *About one hour plus one hour to soak mushrooms*
OVEN TEMPERATURE: *175°C (350°F)*
SERVING SUGGESTION: *Serve with riced potatoes and broccoli.*

SALMON FILLING:
Soak dried mushrooms in warm water about one hour. Cut both kinds of salmon into chunks and puree in a food processor. Chop mushrooms and add with chives. With the motor running, gradually add cream and seasonings. If mixture is too thick, add a little water. Do not overprocess.
Select eight large cabbage leaves. Blanch in boiling water. Drain on paper towels.
Combine fish stock ingredients in a saucepan. Bring to a boil. Cool slightly.
Spread out cabbage leaves. Spoon salmon filling onto leaves. Fold over sides, then roll up to form a packet. Place cabbage rolls in an ovenproof dish. Pour over fish stock to cover. Bake 30 minutes. Drain, reserving cooking liquid.

SAFFRON SAUCE:
In a medium saucepan, whisk together all ingredients for sauce. Bring to a boil, lower heat and simmer until about 2/3 of the original amount remains. If necessary, thicken with cornstarch mixture.

ROOT VEGETABLE MIX:
Sauté root vegetables in butter a few minutes. Stir in parsley and salt.

BEVERAGE SUGGESTION: This is a festive dish with a lot of flavor. Look for a wine to contrast with the dish, a fresh, dry white wine, such as a Sancerre. Or find harmony in a buttery, cask-aged Chardonnay from Australia.

Ingrid Klingspor, Lidköping and Sonja Eriksson, Skara

Fish pudding with pumpkin

FOUR SERVINGS
600 g (1 1/3 lb) grated pumpkin
500 g (1 1/4 lb) ground pike
3 tablespoons flour
1 1/2 dl (2/3 cup) fish stock
1 tablespoon grated horseradish
1 teaspoon salt
1/4 teaspoon freshly ground white pepper
chopped parsley
breadcrumbs
butter

Pike is our local fish, and "pumpkin day" is celebrated in Borås. These two ingredients are united in this unusual dish.

PREPARATION TIME: *90 minutes*
OVEN TEMPERATURE: *175°C (350°F)*
SERVING SUGGESTION: *Serve with boiled potatoes, a salad and melted butter.*

Combine first 7 ingredients and pour into a greased ovenproof dish. Sprinkle with parsley and breadcrumbs. Dot with butter.
Bake 50-60 minutes, depending upon dimensions of baking dish.

Lovisa Johansson, Äspered

SALMON-STUFFED CABBAGE ROLLS WITH SAFFRON SAUCE

Pike burgers

THE COOKBOOK
CONTEST
FIRST PRIZE
INDIVIDUAL
DISHES

FOUR SERVINGS
*500 g (1 1/4 lb) skinless
and boneless pike fillets
125 g (4 oz) salt pork
125 g (4 oz) smoked bacon
1 onion
1 egg
1 dl (1/2 cup) whipping
cream
grated nutmeg
lemon pepper
1/2 teaspoon salt
1/4 teaspoon white pepper
butter*

The combination of pork and freshwater fish can be found in many older cookbooks. In the olden days, people used what they had and often paired fatty pork with lean fish.

PREPARATION TIME: *About one hour*
SERVING SUGGESTION: *Serve with riced potatoes, melted butter and carrots or peas.*

Rinse fish, removing any small bones. Remove rind from pork and cut into small strips. Peel onion and cut into wedges.
Grind fish, pork and onion in a meat grinder or food processor. Stir in egg, cream and spices. Fry a small sample and taste. Adjust seasoning, if necessary.
Form into 8 burgers and fry on both sides in butter over medium heat until golden.

BEVERAGE SUGGESTION: A semi-dry white wine, preferably a German Riesling is good with this dish. Or why not a light beer with moderate to full bitterness?

Annika Dalbert, Åsnebyn

Poached spiny dogfish stuffed with crayfish and spinach

FOUR SERVINGS
*70 g (2 1/2 oz) salmon
fillet
20 crayfish tails
1 teaspoon tomato paste
2 egg yolks
1 dl (1/2 cup)
whipping cream
1/2 teaspoon salt
2 tablespoons minced
onion
1 dl (1/2 cup)
blanched spinach
butter
400 g (14 oz)
spiny dogfish or shark
fillets (preferably 4 fillets)*

*Potatoes:
6 boiled potatoes
1 small carrot
2 garlic cloves
1/2 onion
1/2 red onion
1/2 fennel bulb
100 g (3 oz) sun-dried
tomatoes in oil
1/2 g (pinch) saffron
fish stock (bouillon cube)
salt and pepper*

*Eggplant chips:
1 eggplant*

Spiny dogfish is a favorite of fish lovers and sports fishermen. This is a luxury recipe, and it demands full attention for a perfect result.

TILLAGNINGSTID: *About one hour*
OVEN TEMPERATURE: *225°C (425°F)*

FISH:
Place salmon, crayfish, tomato paste, egg yolks, cream and salt in a food processor and puree until smooth.
Sauté onion with spinach in a little butter.
Split fish fillets horizontally (disregard if very thin). Open and place on a flat surface. Season with salt and pepper. Arrange spinach on fish. Top with fish puree.
Fold over edges and roll up. Wrap tightly in plastic wrap. In a sauté pan, bring a little water to a boil. Add fish packet, cover and simmer slowly for about 20 minutes.

POTATOES:
Slice potatoes, carrot and garlic. Cut onions and fennel into wedges. Sauté in some oil from the tomatoes. Stir in saffron. Shred sundried tomatoes and add.
Add water to almost cover. Add a small amount of fish stock and salt. Simmer 10-15 minutes. Season with salt and pepper.

EGGPLANT CHIPS:
Thinly slice eggplant. Deep-fry until golden. Drain on paper towels.

BEVERAGE SUGGESTION: A light luxurious wine suits luxury food. A dry white Bordeaux with class or a Sauvignon Blanc from New Zealand both have the freshness to match the dogfish and the crayfish. Wine connoisseurs would perhaps prefer a Sauvignon Blanc from Steiermark in Austria.

Pierre Karlsson, Trollhättan

Pike burgers

Burbot Fricassee

FOUR SERVINGS
2 dl (3/4 cup) water
1 fish bouillon cube
1 small fennel bulb
1 small leek
2 dl (3/4 cup)
crème fraiche or
whipping cream
400 g (14 oz)
chanterelles or
other mushrooms
600 g (1 1/3 lb)
skinless and boneless
burbot fillets
chopped chives
chopped parsley

Burbot can be difficult to prepare, so many choose other fish. Buy skinless and boneless fillets and enjoy this interesting fish. Actually, almost any kind of fish can be used in this recipe.

PREPARATION TIME: *About 30 minutes*
SERVING SUGGESTION: *Serve with rice or potatoes.*

In a sauté pan, heat water and add bouillon cube. Shred fennel and leek. Simmer in bouillon until tender. Whisk in crème fraiche. In another pan, sauté mushrooms without added fat until all liquid has evaporated. Transfer to sauté pan. Cut fish into 1 cm (1/2") thick chunks and add. Simmer until cooked through, about 5 minutes. Sprinkle with chives and parsley, and serve directly from the pan.

BEVERAGE SUGGESTION: A dry white wine is good with this tasty fish fricassee. Choose a young Chardonnay.

Gunilla Wahrnberg, Ed

Late summer fish stew

FOUR SERVINGS
2 large baking potatoes
2 tablespoons olive oil
salt and pepper
2 dl (3/4 cup) fish stock
2 dl (3/4 cup) white wine
2 dl (3/4 cup) whipping
cream
2 dl (3/4 cup) crème
fraiche or whipping cream
2 g (1/8 teaspoon) saffron
500 g (1 lb) mussels
1 bunch radishes
1 large carrot
2 red onions
200 g (7 oz) monkfish fillets
200 g (7 oz) skinless eel fillets
200 g (7 oz) spiny dogfish or
shark fillets
2 teaspoons cornstarch
stirred into 1 tablespoon
cold water (optional)
chopped chives
lemon wedges

Fish stews are always beautiful and fun to make. Fillets do not add as much flavor as whole fish, but they do save time. The types of fish used in this stew are not always easy to find, but the recipe works well with most kinds of white freshwater and saltwater fish.

PREPARATION TIME: *About 45 minutes*
OVEN TEMPERATURE: *225°C (425°F)*

Brush and rinse potatoes. Cut into large wedges and place on an oiled baking tray. Sprinkle with salt and pepper and drizzle with olive oil. Bake about 20 minutes, turning halfway through.
In a saucepan, combine fish stock and wine and reduce over high heat until about half the original amount remains. Add cream and reduce by 1/3. Whisk in crème fraiche and saffron. Season with salt and pepper.
Scrub mussels well, discarding any which are open or broken. Place in a saucepan in a little lightly salted water. Cover and boil until all are opened. Discard any which have not opened.
Clean and trim radishes. Peel carrot, halve lengthwise, then slice thinly. Peel onion and cut into thin wedges.
Cut monkfish diagonally into 1 cm (1/2") slices. Cut eel and dogfish into eight pieces of equal size. Grill monkfish in a hot grill pan. Sauté eel and dogfish on both sides in olive oil.
Sauté vegetables in a deep frying pan, then add dogfish and eel. Add sauce and bring to a boil. If using additional cream instead of crème fraiche, thicken with cornstarch mixture.
Arrange potatoes and mussels in the bottom of deep plates. Ladle over fish stew and top with grilled monkfish. Garnish with chives and lemon wedges.

BEVERAGE SUGGESTION: A fresh, young, dry white wine is good with this fish stew.

Jonas Runnberg, Gothenburg

BURBOT FRICASSEE

Plaice in white wine sauce

FOUR SERVINGS
White wine sauce:
2 dl (3/4 cup) vegetable
bouillon
2 dl (3/4 cup) white wine
3 dl (1 1/4 cups)
whipping cream
1 teaspoon salt
1 teaspoon cumin
1/2 teaspoon ground ginger
2 teaspoons cornstarch
stirred into 1 tablespoon
cold water

Fish:
1 medium leek, trimmed
and sliced
8 plaice fillets
8 slices bacon

40 g (1/3 cup) grated
parmesan cheese

Fish, bacon and onion are a familiar combination in the modern kitchen. The seasoning in this sauce is unusual for fish.

PREPARATION TIME: *About 50 minutes*
OVEN TEMPERATURE: *200°C (400°F)*
SERVING SUGGESTION: *Serve with new potatoes*
and tiny peas.

In a saucepan, combine fish stock and wine, and reduce over high heat until about 2 dl (3/4 cup) remains. Add cream and simmer until slightly thickened, about 35 minutes. Add seasonings. Remove from heat. Add cornstarch mixture and cook until thickened.
Grease an ovenproof dish. Sprinkle sliced leek over the bottom. Bake 10 minutes. Roll up fish fillets, inside out, and wrap each in bacon. Arrange on leeks. Stir cheese into sauce and pour over fish. Bake 20 minutes.

BEVERAGE SUGGESTION: The trendy seasoning of the fish is good with a modern, fruity "new world" white wine. Try a Sauvignon Blanc or Chenin Blanc from South Africa.

Birgitta Dahlberg, Nacka

Summer mackerel

FOUR SERVINGS
16 tiny carrots
16 tiny parsnips
8 fresh mackerel
fillets, about 1 kg
(2 1/4 lb)
1 teaspoon salt
1 dl (1/2 cup) dry
breadcrumbs
2 tablespoons butter
2 tablespoons
chopped dill

"In the light of the morning sun, mackerel shines in green, black and mother of pearl. It's the most beautiful fish found along the coast, and also one of the best and most nourishing," says restaurateur Bengt Petersen in his book, *Bohus fish and shellfish.* The best fish is the one you caught yourself, prepared at once.

PREPARATION TIME: *About 40 minutes*
SERVING SUGGESTION: *Serve with new potatoes, dill, lemon wedges and*
large rounds of crispbread and butter.

Rinse and clean vegetables. Blanch in lightly salted water, then plunge into cold water. Dip fillets in salted crumbs, then fry in butter over medium heat, about 2 minutes per side.
Sauté vegetables lightly in butter, then sprinkle with dill.
Serve immediately.

BEVERAGE SUGGESTION: A light beer with medium bitterness is good with dish.

Jonas Runnberg, Gothenburg

Grilled ocean catfish with spring vegetables

FOUR SERVINGS
8 almond potatoes
2 black salsify
2 celery stalks

Sauce:
10 spring onions
2 carrots
40 g (1 1/2 oz) fresh ginger
8 dl (3 1/3 cups) chicken stock
50 g (3 tablespoons)
unsalted butter
salt and pepper

1 beet
corn oil

4 skinless and boneless
ocean catfish fillets,
about 80 g (3 oz) each

Ocean catfish is an especially "meaty" fish. Other kinds of fish can be used in this recipe, even lamb and chicken.

PREPARATION TIME: *One hour*

Clean potatoes and cut in half lengthwise. Peel and halve black salsify (place in acidulated water after peeling). Cut celery into 5 cm (2") lengths. Blanch vegetables in salted water.
Halve spring onions lengthwise. Peel and grate carrots and ginger. In a saucepan, sauté ginger and onions in a little butter until soft. Add stock and carrot. Reduce over low heat until half the original amount remains. Whisk in butter and season with salt and pepper. Pour into a food processor and puree until smooth. Strain.
Peel and shred beet. Heat oil to 175°C (350°F). Deep-fry until crisp.

BEVERAGE SUGGESTION: The hearty fish and silky black salsify (one of wine's best friends) go well with a medium-bodied red wine or a more flavorful dry white wine.

Anders Liss and Daniel Timgren, Skövde

Flounder roulades with fresh tomato sauce

FOUR SERVINGS
600 g (1 1/3 lb) flounder fillets
1/2 teaspoon salt

Sauce:
1 large onion
1 garlic clove
1 tablespoon olive oil
3 tablespoons tomato paste
2 tomatoes, peeled, seeded
and chopped
2 dl (3/4 cup) fish stock
2 dl (3/4 cup) white wine
1 tomato, thinly sliced

Vegetable rice:
2 dl (3/4 cup) rice
1/2 teaspoon salt
4 dl (1 2/3 cups) water
8 snow peas
1 red bell pepper
olive oil
chives

Sole, flounder, brill and plaice are all flat fish.
The most expensive is sole; the cheapest, plaice, with the fastest cooking time, but a softer flesh.
Flounder is somewhere in between.
It's both reasonably priced and delicious.

PREPARATION TIME: *About 45 minutes*
OVEN TEMPERATURE: *175°C (350°F)*

Grease an ovenproof dish. Salt fillets, then roll up and place in the dish. Cover with foil and bake about 15 minutes.
Peel and chop onion and garlic. Sauté in olive oil. Add tomato paste and chopped tomatoes. Pour over stock and bouillon and reduce until slightly thickened. Strain. Just before serving, add tomato and heat through.
Cook rice with salt and water until just done, about 25 minutes. Shred snow peas and bell pepper. Sauté in olive oil, then stir into rice.
Spoon rice onto a serving platter. Top with fish roulades, then pour sauce all around. Garnish with whole chives.

BEVERAGE SUGGESTION: Serve with a dry or semi-dry white wine to offset the acidity of the tomato sauce.

Jonas Runnberg, Gothenburg

GRILLED OCEAN CATFISH WITH SPRING VEGETABLES

Cod with bacon and leek

FOUR SERVINGS
*600 g (1 1/3 lb) thick
cod fillets, skin on
3 tablespoons
coarse salt
150 g (5 oz) sliced
bacon
1 medium leek
2 tablespoons
chopped parsley*

This recipe is originally from Gullholmen. Restaurateur Bengt Petersen brought it to a course at Gerlesborg School. That's when Meta Bruto adopted it and gave it a modern touch with bacon and leek.

PREPARATION TIME: *About 30 minutes plus two hours in the refrigerator*
SERVING SUGGESTION: *Serve with boiled potatoes.*

Sprinkle fish with salt. Cover with plastic wrap and refrigerate about 2 hours. Rinse off salt, then simmer in water to cover for about 8 minutes.
While fish is cooking, fry bacon until crisp.
Clean and slice leek. Sauté until soft.
Arrange fish on a serving platter. Top with bacon and leeks. Sprinkle with parsley.

BEVERAGE SUGGESTION: Cod is a flavorful fish, and when served in this manner, a medium-bodied red wine with moderate tannin is the best choice. Select a lighter red Bordeaux or a red wine from the Loire valley or northern Italy. Serve lightly chilled.

Meta Bruto, Bovallstrand

Haddock with ocean crayfish

FOUR SERVINGS
*4 large haddock fillets,
700-800 g (1 1/2 - 1 3/4 lb)
2 dl (3/4 cup) crayfish
or fish stock
2 dl (3/4 cup) beer
1 kg (2 1/4 lb) potatoes
2 parsnips, about 150 g (5 oz)
2 dl (3/4 cup) coffee cream
or half and half
salt and pepper
4 tablespoons (1/4 cup)
capers
4 tablespoons (1/4 cup)
chopped pickled beets
unsalted butter
dill fronds
4 cooked ocean crayfish*

Many feel that haddock is a more refined fish than cod. It is even better when served "English-style" and garnished with whole crayfish.

PREPARATION TIME: *About 45 minutes*
OVEN TEMPERATURE: *175°C (350°F)*

Roll up fillets and place in a greased ovenproof dish. Add stock and beer to cover. Boil potatoes and parsnips and mash. Add cream to desired consistency. Season with salt and pepper.
Bake until fish is opaque, about 20 minutes.
Spoon a mound of vegetable puree onto each plate. Top with fish.
Sauté capers and beets in a generous amount of butter and pour over fish.
Garnish with dill fronds and crayfish.

BEVERAGE SUGGESTION: This classic fish dish can be served with a light beer or a dry white wine.

Jonas Runnberg, Gothenburg

Cod with bacon and leeks

Gothenburg-style whiting

SIX SERVINGS
1 bunch parsley
20 small whiting
1 1/2 tablespoons butter
2 tablespoons flour
2 dl (3/4 cup) fish stock
1 dl (1/2 cup) white wine
1 dl (1/2 cup)
whipping cream

This dish is a Gothenburg specialty. It is served to adults with patience and a side dish for skin and bones.

PREPARATION TIME: *35 minutes*
SERVING SUGGESTION: *Serve with boiled potatoes.*

Coarsely chop parsley and blanch in boiling water for a few seconds. Clean fish, cutting off heads and tails. Rinse thoroughly. Simmer fish in lightly salted water to cover for 5-10 minutes, according to size. Remove from cooking water and keep warm. Melt butter, stir in flour and slowly add fish stock, wine and cream. Simmer until thick. Stir in chopped parsley.

BEVERAGE SUGGESTION: Whiting has a very mild, nutty flavor. For that reason, any beverage should not be too dominating. A light, fresh and dry white wine from Italy or a cool Pilsner are the best choices.

Familjen Eliasson, Gothenburg

Fresh cod lutefisk

TWELWE SERVINGS
3 1/3 kg (7 1/4 lb)
fresh cod
salt
2 liters (quarts) water
40 g (3 tablespoons)
baking soda
250 g (9 oz) slaked lime

Most Swedish lutefisk is made from ling. Pollack and cod are used in Norway and in northern Sweden. Homemade lutefisk can serve as the basis for many dinners. Whether it is served with bechamel sauce or melted butter, in addition to boiled potatoes, is a matter of taste.

PREPARATION TIME: *About 16 days*

Rinse cod, then clean and rinse again. Remove skin and bones. (Use head and bones to make stock). Rub fillets with salt and place in a glass dish. Refrigerate. Salt draws moisture from fish and forms brine. Pour off brine daily. Wipe dish dry and rub fillets with salt every day. Repeat daily for one week. Now the fillets are ready for "luting". Bring water and soda to a boil. Cool. Sprinkle a layer of lime in the bottom of a wooden tray or plastic basin. Cut fish in half and layer with lime, ending with lime. Pour over cold soda mixture. Press down with a plate. The fish must be completely covered. After 48 hours, pour off soda mixture and cover with water. Change water every day for at least one week before serving. Lutefisk shrinks when cooked, so count on 500 g (1 lb) per person. Rinse fish before simmering in water about 8 minutes. Serve immediately with strong mustard.

BEVERAGE SUGGESTION: Many kinds of beverages can be served with lutefisk. Most prefer a dark beer with a relatively high alcohol content or a lighter, low alcohol beer are the usual choices, but it also can be served with a red Bordeaux or a sweet Sauternes.

Familjen Eliasson, Gothenburg

GOTHENBURG-STYLE WHITING

Trout bundles on a bed of spinach

THREE SERVINGS
Puff pastry:
200 g (7 oz) unsalted butter
4 dl (1 2/3 cups) flour
1 1/2 dl (2/3 cup) water

Creamed spinach:
275 g (10 oz) frozen chopped spinach
1 dl (1/2 cup) milk
50 g (1/2 cup) grated Swiss cheese
1/4 teaspoon salt
1/8 teaspoon ground paprika
pinch white pepper
pinch grated nutmeg
25 g (1 1/2 tablespoons) butter
1/2 dl (3 1/2 table-spoons) flour
1/2 dl (3 1/2 table-spoons) whipping cream

250 g (9 oz) skinless and boneless fresh or smoked trout fillets
2 tablespoons chopped dill
1/2 teaspoon herb-seasoned salt
1/4 teaspoon lemon pepper
1/8 teaspoon thyme

1 egg yolk

After the "pie-boom" of the 1980s, we now serve all possible varieties of rolls, packets and bundles. Food enclosed in pastry retains all its juiciness and flavor, and many of these dishes are good both hot and cold. One little drawback is that the crispy casing is a real calorie bomb.

PREPARATION TIME: *80 minutes plus one hour if making puff pastry from scratch*
OVEN TEMPERATURE: *225°C (425°F)*
SERVING SUGGESTION: *Riced potatoes and buttered carrots*

PUFF PASTRY:
Make in a food processor, or in a mixing bowl. Cut 1/4 of the butter into most of the flour until mixture resembles coarse meal. Add water and mix until dough sticks together and pulls away from sides of bowl. Form into a ball, then flatten.
Roll pastry into a square. Slice butter and place in center. Fold four corners of pastry over butter, covering completely, to make a new square. Turn pastry, so that seams are underneath. Roll out carefully, keeping butter enclosed in pastry. Fold pastry into thirds. Roll out again. Fold pastry into thirds in other direction. Let pastry rest in refrigerator 10 minutes. Repeat rolling and folding two more times. Cover and let pastry rest in refrigerator until needed.

CREAMED SPINACH:
Defrost spinach in a saucepan with milk. Stir frequently so milk does not begin to boil. When spinach is completely defrosted, add cheese and seasonings. Knead butter and flour together and add to spinach to thicken. Then add cream. Cover and simmer about 5 minutes. Cool slightly.

BEFORE BAKING:
Spread a thin layer of creamed spinach in an ovenproof dish just large enough.
Cut trout fillets in the center. Sprinkle with dill and seasonings.
Remove pastry from refrigerator and divide into four parts. Roll each into thin squares. Divide half the remaining spinach on the squares, then spoon remaining spinach over fish. Roll up. Place a fish roll on each pastry square. Pull corners up over the fish and twist. Brush with egg yolk.
Place bundles on bed of spinach and bake about 30 minutes on lowest oven shelf.

BEVERAGE SUGGESTION: This beautiful, light dish goes well with a dry sparkling wine – for a festive meal, serve Champagne!

Christina von Brömssen, Hjo

Chicken with shrimp

FOUR PORTIONS
1 small leek
1-2 garlic cloves
*4 boneless and skinless
chicken breasts
rapeseed oil
lemon pepper
2 tomatoes
200 g (7 oz) fresh
mushrooms
2 dl (3/4 cup) crème fraiche
or whipping cream
soy sauce
4 tablespoons (1/4 cup)
capers
2-3 tablespoons sherry
or red wine (optional)
2-3 drops Tabasco sauce
100-200 g (4-7 oz)
peeled shrimp*

Sometimes we salt food without thinking, but it isn't always necessary. In this dish, the capers add enough salt. Here is a slightly Swedish version of the Chinese dish, chicken with shrimp.

PREPARATION TIME: *30 minutes*
SERVING SUGGESTION: *Serve with boiled rice and a tomato-leek salad with a dressing of cider vinegar and a little sugar.*

Rinse and shred leek. Mince garlic.
Cut chicken breasts into chunks. Brown leek in oil, then set aside. Brown chicken and garlic, then return leek to pan. Season with lemon pepper. Cut tomatoes into wedges, slice mushrooms and add. Stir in crème fraiche. Season with soy sauce and capers. Add wine and Tabasco. Simmer a few minutes.
Add shrimp and heat through. Do not allow sauce to boil after adding shrimp.

Elisabeth Stigen-Salén, Mellerud

Duck in lingonberry sauce

FOUR SERVINGS
Potato-celeriac puree:
*10 potatoes
300 g (10 oz) celeriac
2 dl (3/4 cup)
coffee cream
or half and half
3 tablespoons butter
salt and pepper*

*4 duck breasts,
about 600 g (1 1/3 lb)*

Sauce:
*5 dl (2 cups)
whipping cream
1 dl (1/2 cup) duck
or beef stock
1 dl (1/2 cup)
lingonberries
salt and pepper
pinch sugar*

chopped parsley

According to Dr. Hagdahl, ducks should be cooked as soon as they are slaughtered, because they do not benefit from aging as other varieties of game usually do.

PREPARATION TIME: *One hour*
OVEN TEMPERATURE: *250 °C (475 °F)*
SERVING SUGGESTION: *Serve with lingonberry compote.*

Peel potatoes and celeriac. Cut into chunks and cook separately in lightly salted water until tender. Drain, then combine and mash. Add cream, butter, salt and pepper. Beat until fluffy, then pipe puree along the edges of an ovenproof dish.
Score fat on duck breasts, then brown, skin side down. Drain fat (and use to fry potatoes). Turn and brown on other side. Transfer to ovenproof dish.
Deglaze pan with a little water. Add cream and stock. Reduce over high heat until about half the original amount remains. Add lingonberries. Season with salt, pepper and a pinch of sugar.
Pour sauce over duck breasts and bake about 10 minutes. They should still be pink inside. To serve, spoon a mound of puree on each plate. Top with a duck breast. Pour sauce all around. Garnish with chopped parsley.

BEVERAGE SUGGESTION: With its generous amount of cream and hearty flavor, this dish needs a red wine with pronounced tannin. A red Bordeaux, a wine from Madiran in southwest France or a good quality Cabernet Sauvignon from South Africa all work vell with this dish.

Gunnar Malm, Gothenburg

Stuffed chicken rolls
with potato-celeriac compote

EIGHT SERVINGS
*2 chickens, about 1 kg
(2 1/4 lb) each
8 thin slices smoked ham
fleur de sel-gourmet salt and
black pepper*

*Potato-celeriac compote:
600 g (1 1/3 lb) potatoes
300 g (10 oz) celeriac
1 dl (1/2 cup) whipping cream
3 egg yolks
salt and white pepper
4 spring roll wrappers
melted butter*

*Roasted garlic sauce:
2 heads garlic
4 shallots
corn oil
6 dl (2 1/2 cups) chicken stock
2 teaspoons cornstarch stirred
into 1 tablespoon cold water
salt and white pepper
white wine vinegar*

*200 g (7 oz) celeriac
corn oil*

Timely trends…roasted garlic, deep-fried shredded vegetables, rolls and packets. Remember that the best chickens are free-range birds.

PREPARATION TIME: *80 minutes*
OVEN TEMPERATURE: *Schnitzels, 150°C (300°F);
everything else, 200°C (400°F)*

Remove all skin from chickens, keeping it as "whole" as possible. Cut out breasts. Slice breasts horizontally and open up to form "schnitzels". Remove leg bone and scrape clean. Remove all meat from carcass and chop.
Place two slices of ham on each schnitzel. Arrange chopped meat on top. Season with salt and pepper. Roll up tightly and wrap in chicken skin. Bake 20-25 minutes.
Peel potatoes and celeriac and cut into chunks. Boil until tender. Drain and steam slightly. Mash coarsely. Heat cream and add. Beat in two egg yolks. Season with salt and pepper. Spread mixture over spring roll wrappers and roll up tightly. Brush edges with egg yolk to seal. Just before serving, brush with butter and bake about 15 minutes.
Halve garlic heads horizontally and bake 15-20 minutes. Mince shallots and sauté in a little oil. Add stock and roasted garlic. Simmer until half the original amount remains. Thicken with cornstarch mixture. Season with salt, pepper and a few drops of vinegar. Puree in a food processor until smooth.
Deep-fry celeriac in hot oil. Drain on paper towels.
Reheat chicken rolls, slice and serve with potato-celeriac rolls and shredded celeriac.

BEVERAGE SUGGESTION: A young, flavorful dry white wine suits this dish. For a trendy choice, try a wine made from Viognier grapes, which are being grown more and more in Europe, Australia and California.

Eliasson family, Gothenburg

LÄCKÖ CASTLE

Roast partridge stuffed with croutons

FOUR SERVINGS
4 slices soft white bread
butter
4 partridges
2 onions
10 sage leaves, chopped
300 g (10 oz) sliced bacon
4 dl (1 2/3 cups) chicken stock
4 dl (1 2/3 cups) white wine
1/2 - 1 dl (1/3 cup)
whipping cream

Many hunters with retrievers like to shoot partridges. Others prefer just to eat them.

PREPARATION TIME: *One hour*
SERVING SUGGESTION: *Serve with buttered carrots, brussels sprouts and rice pilaf or potatoes.*

Cut bread into cubes and brown in butter until crispy. Remove giblets from partridges and cube. Chop onion and sage. Sauté giblets, half the onion and sage in butter 10-15 minutes. Mix with bread cubes. Stuff birds with this mixture. Wrap birds in bacon and tie.
Brown birds in butter with remaining onion. Transfer to a large pot. Add stock and wine, cover and simmer about 30 minutes. Remove birds and keep warm. Strain cooking liquid and stir in cream. Simmer about 5 minutes before serving.

Olav Hoheisel, Falköping

Steamed clay pot pheasant with white wine and fruit

THREE - FOUR
SERVINGS
1 pheasant, about
1 kg (2 1/4 lb)
6 potatoes
1 large leek
2 carrots
100 g (4 oz) celeriac
2 parsnips
300 g (10 oz)
jerusalem artichokes
7 dl (3 cups) semi-
dry white wine

A clay pot is inexpensive and easy to use. The food cooks on its own, and the results are always juicy and flavorful. Lift the lid, and the aroma of pheasant, wine and root vegetables is just tantalizing.
Important to know: The entire pot must soak in cold water for at least 15 minutes before using, and the cooking time is longer than conventional methods.

PREPARATION TIME: *Two hours*
OVEN TEMPERATURE: *225°C (425°F)*
SERVING SUGGESTION: *Serve with freshly baked bread.*

Rinse pheasant, inside and out.
Dry with paper towels. Prepare clay pot as stated above.
Cut vegetables into batons. Place in pot with pheasant. Sprinkle with salt and pepper. Add wine.
Bake about 90 minutes.

BEVERAGE SUGGESTION: When flavorful pheasant is cooked in white wine, it matches well with a light red wine, such as Beaujolais, or a slightly aromatic white wine, such as an Alsatian Gewurztraminer.

Gunnar Malm, Gothenburg

ROAST PARTRIDGE STUFFED WITH CROUTONS

Citrus-marinated breast of turkey

FOUR – FIVE SERVINGS
*500 g (1 1/4 lb)
fresh turkey breast
1 dl (1/3 cup) orange
juice concentrate
1/2 chicken bouillon
cube*

*Sauce:
2 tablespoons water
1/2 tablespoon flour
1 dl (1/2 cup)
whipping cream
juices from roasting
salt and pepper*

*Red onion salsa:
3 red onions
1 tablespoon olive oil
2 tablespoons
balsamic vinegar
2 tablespoons honey
2 tablespoons
chopped ginger
1 dl (scant 1/2 cup)
red wine
1/2 teaspoon salt
1/4 teaspoon
black pepper*

It has taken a long time for turkey to gain entry to the Swedish kitchen. It has been in Europe since the 16th century, and Kajsa Warg had many turkey recipes in her cookbook from the 18th century. But it is only now that we really appreciate this lean, protein-rich meat. The meat has a mild flavor and invites experimenting with new recipes.

PREPARATION TIME: *About one hour plus marinating overnight*
OVEN TEMPERATURE: *200°C (400°F)*
SERVING SUGGESTION: *Potato wedges (preferably flavored with garlic and rosemary) and green beans with grated parmesan.*

Place turkey breast in a roasting bag. Add orange juice concentrate. Crumble bouillon cube and add. Tie. Marinate in refrigerator about 10 hours, turning bag several times.
Bake in bag until internal temperature reaches 80°C (175°F). Reserve juices for sauce.

SAUCE:
In a saucepan, whisk water and flour until smooth. Add cream and juices from roasting bag. Simmer 3 minutes. Season with salt and pepper.

RED ONION SALSA:
Thinly slice onion and sauté in oil over low heat until soft, about 5 minutes. Add vinegar, honey, ginger, red wine, salt and pepper. Simmer over low heat about 10 minutes.

*This slightly exotic sauce is a good alternative to the above:
2 dl (3/4 cup) commercial dessert sauce made with mango, passion fruit, orange or lemon. (These often can be found with ice cream toppings.)
2 dl (3/4 cup) whipping cream
1 chicken bouillon cube
In a saucepan, bring all ingredients to a boil. Serve immediately.*

BEVERAGE SUGGESTION: This mild, slightly acidic dish is best with white wine. Choose a dry, spicy Alsace or a semi-dry Riesling Kabinett/ Spätlese from Germany.

Meta Bruto, Bovallstrand

Grilled ostrich with sautéed vegetables

FOUR SERVINGS
200 g (7 oz) oyster mushrooms
2 tablespoons butter
150 g spring onions
1 zucchini
1 yellow bell pepper
1 red bell pepper
150 g (5 oz) snow peas
1 teaspoon salt
1/2 teaspoon
freshly ground pepper
1/2 teaspoon thyme
2 dl (3/4 cup) whipping cream
600 g (1 1/3 lb) filet of ostrich
1 tablespoon olive oil
1 teaspoon salt
1/2 teaspoon pepper

The number of ostrich farmers increases every year. Ostrich has been eaten for centuries in other cultures, but it is a new dish for Swedes. Ostrich is lean and resembles beef in flavor.

PREPARATION TIME: *About 45 minutes plus possible soaking of beans overnight*

SERVING SUGGESTION: *Serve with potatoes or pasta.*

Cube mushrooms, cut onions into 5 cm (2") lengths, thinly slice zucchini and cut peppers into chunks. Cut snow peas diagonally into thirds.
Sauté mushrooms in butter, then add onions, zucchini and peppers and cook a few minutes more. Add snow peas.
Season with salt, pepper and thyme. Add cream and simmer until slightly thickened.
Cut the meat into 1 cm (1/2") slices. Brush with olive oil, then sprinkle with salt and pepper.
Grill or sauté meat about 2 minutes per side over medium heat. Serve with vegetable mix.

Marinated vegetables
1 dl (1/2 cup) black beans
6 dl (2 1/2 cups) water
1 red onion
1 large red bell pepper
1 large yellow bell pepper
200 g (7 oz) snow peas
2 teaspoons vinegar
2 tablespoons olive oil
1 teaspoon salt
chopped fresh basil

An alternative:
Soak beans in water to cover overnight. Drain, then cook in lightly salted water until tender. Cut vegetables into chunks and blanch in boiling water. Immediately plunge into cold water. Whisk together vinegar, oil and salt. Pour over the vegetables, add basil and toss well.

Ulrika Fröberg, Tollered

Turkey Viennese

FOUR SERVINGS
600 g (1 1/3 lb) turkey breast
4 thin slices smoked ham
4 slices Gruyere cheese,
about 60 g (2 oz)
4 tablespoons (1/4 cup) flour
2 eggs, lightly beaten
4 tablespoons (1/4 cup)
dry breadcrumbs
8 medium potatoes,
700 g (1 3/4 lb)
100 g (3 oz) unsalted butter
1/2 teaspoon salt
1/4 teaspoon ground
white pepper

Veal or chicken with ham and cheese is known as "cordon bleu"; when breaded and fried, it is called "viennoise". This is a combination of those two dishes made with turkey breast.

PREPARATION TIME: *About 45 minutes*

SERVING SUGGESTION: *Serve with lemon slices, capers, melted butter and tiny peas. A hearty sauce based on natural juices is also good. Make it with veal stock or a bouillon cube.*

Place the turkey breast on a cutting board, flat side down. Cut horizontally into four slices of equal size. Place each slice between sheets of plastic wrap and pound lightly.
Place a slice of ham and cheese on each. Fold meat over cheese.
Dip first in flour, then in beaten egg and finally into breadcrumbs.
Peel potatoes and cut into thin slices. Fry in butter.
Season with salt and pepper.
Fry meat in butter about 4 minutes per side.
The meat is done when cheese begins to run out.

BEVERAGE SUGGESTION: A dry, slightly spicy white wine is good with this dish. Try a Tokay Pinot Gris from Alsace or a green Veltliner from Austria.

Jonas Runnberg, Gothenburg

GRILLED OSTRICH WITH SAUTÉED VEGETABLES

Breast of eider duck with parsley

FOUR SERVINGS
4 eider duck breasts
1 tablespoon corn oil
salt and freshly ground
black pepper
1 dl (1/2 cup)
chopped parsley
1 tablespoon
light cream cheese
1 shallot, minced

Jerusalem artichokes:
200 g (7 oz) jerusalem
artichokes
3 dl (1 1/4 cups) light cream
salt

Sauce:
1 shallot, minced
1 small carrot, minced
1 tablespoon corn oil
4 dl (1 2/3 cups) beef stock
1 dl (1/2 cup) blackberries,
plus a few for garnish
salt and freshly ground
black pepper

Neither Carl Emil Hagdahl nor Gustafva Björklund included eider duck in their cookbooks. Eider has mostly been considered emergency food. Use the breasts with parsley and jerusalem artichokes for a new flavor experience.

PREPARATION TIME: *45 minutes*   OVEN TEMPERATURE: *175°C (350°F)*
SERVING SUGGESTION: *Serve with roasted potatoes or potato wedges with skin and a garnish of parsley.*

EIDER DUCK:
Brown breasts in a hot pan filmed with oil. Season with salt and pepper.
In a food processor, mix parsley and cheese until green, then add shallot, salt and pepper.
Spread a layer of parsley mixture on each breast. Bake about 15 minutes, until they have reached an internal temperature of 70°C (160°F). Let rest 15 minutes before slicing.

JERUSALEM ARTICHOKES:
Peel and cut the jerusalem artichokes into chunks. Simmer in cream until soft. Season with salt.

SAUCE:
Sauté onion and carrot in oil until soft, then add stock and berries. Simmer 15 minutes, then puree in a food processor until smooth, and press through a sieve. Season with salt and pepper. Just before serving, add a few whole berries to the sauce. If berries are very sour, add a teaspoon of honey.

Lisbeth Zettenius, Strömstad

Chicken in mustard sauce

FOUR SERVINGS
4 chicken breasts
1/2 - 1 teaspoon salt
1/4 teaspoon freshly ground
black pepper
2 tomatoes
1 shallot
3-4 tablespoons chopped basil
4 slices Swiss cheese

Sauce:
1 shallot
2 dl (3/4 cup) whipping cream
2 dl (3/4 cup) chicken stock
rind and juice from 1 lemon
1 tablespoon Dijon-style mustard
2 tablespoons sweet-strong Skåne
mustard
salt and pepper

Mild chicken breast is a good foil for flavorful accompaniments and a creamy sauce. Breast meat dries out easily. It remains juicy in this recipe because it is not browned first.

PREPARATION TIME: *About 30 minutes*
OVEN TEMPERATURE: *175°C (350°F)*
SERVING SUGGESTION: *Serve with boiled rice, colored with tumeric and colorful vegetables.*

Place chicken breasts in a greased ovenproof dish. Season with salt and pepper. Chop tomato and mince shallot. Sprinkle over chicken, then sprinkle with basil.
Top with cheese. Bake about 20 minutes.

SAUCE:
Chop onion and sauté in oil until soft. Add cream, stock and lemon rind. Simmer about 10 minutes.
Add both mustards, lemon juice, salt and pepper.

Margareta Bercu, Grimsås

BREAST OF EIDER DUCK WITH PARSLEY

Pasta with saffron-chile sauce

FOUR SERVINGS
Sauce:
1 shallot
2 tablespoons chopped lemongrass
1 tablespoon rapeseed oil
1/2 g (pinch) saffron
rind and juice from 1 lemon
4 dl (1 2/3 cups) vegetable stock
1 tablespoon sugar
2 teaspoons cornstarch dissolved in
1 tablespoon cold water
salt and freshly ground black pepper
1 tablespoon butter

Pasta:
400 g (14 oz) fresh pasta, such as
Mafaldini
1 red onion
2 red bell peppers
6 savoy cabbage leaves
1 red chile pepper
1 tablespoon olive oil

Many varieties of fresh chiles are available. Experiment with all the different colors and flavors. But – remove all the white ribs and seeds – that's where most of the heat is. Rinse you hands and don't touch your eyes. It can really sting.

PREPARATION TIME: *30 minutes*

SAUCE:
Mince shallot and lemongrass and sauté in oil with saffron and lemon rind until shiny. Add stock, sugar and half the lemon juice. Simmer 10 minutes, then add cornstarch mixture. Cook until thickened. Season with salt, pepper, lemon juice and more sugar, if needed. Strain. Bring to a boil and whisk in the butter.

PASTA:
Cook pasta according to package directions. Plunge into cold water. Drain.
Shred onion and peppers, cut cabbage into squares, remove seeds and ribs from chile and mince. Sauté onion, peppers, cabbage and chile in olive oil until shiny. Stir a little sauce into the drained pasta, mixing well until pasta is warm. Serve immediately with remaining sauce.

BEVERAGE SUGGESTION: Serve with a dry white wine, preferably an Italian Soave.

Bosse and Nina Markendahl, Skee

Root vegetable gratin

FOUR SERVINGS
1 medium cooked
rutabaga (raw weight
about 500 g (1 1/4 lb)
3 large carrots
1 medium leek
3 onions
3 medium potatoes
2 large parsnips
1 teaspoon dried thyme
3-4 tablespoons chopped
fresh parsley

Sauce:
4 dl (1 2/3 cups) water
2 vegetable bouillon cubes
1/4 teaspoon white pepper
1 tablespoon butter
1 1/2 tablespoons flour

Before the potato conquered Scandinavia, rutabaga was one of our basic everyday foods. It gives flavor and substance to this vegetable gratin.

PREPARATION TIME: *About 45 minutes plus 40-45 minutes for cooking the rutabaga*
OVEN TEMPERATURE: *225 °C (450 °F)*
SERVING SUGGESTION: *Serve on its own or with smoked fish or ham.*

Cut cooked rutabaga into batons and arrange on the bottom of a greased ovenproof dish.
Thinly slice all other vegetables and layer with thyme and parsley over rutabaga.
Combine sauce ingredients in a saucepan. Whisk until smooth, then simmer 3 minutes. Pour over vegetables.
Bake on the lowest oven shelf 40-50 minutes.

BEVERAGE SUGGESTION: Choose the beverage according to the other dishes. A dry or semi-dry, fruity white wine goes well with smoked fish or ham. Try a New Zealand Riesling.

Bernt Wernlund, Kinna

PASTA WITH SAFFRON-CHILE SAUCE

Beet burgers with lentils and red-speckled yellow pepper sauce

FOUR SERVINGS
Burgers:
1 shallot
2 garlic cloves
3 fresh beets
1 dl (1/2 cup) red lentils
4 dl (1 2/3 cups) vegetable stock
100 g (1 cup) day-old white bread crumbs
salt and freshly ground black pepper
olive oil

Sauce:
1 onion
1 garlic clove
1 yellow bell pepper
1 tablespoon olive oil
1/4 teaspoon tumeric
4 dl (1 2/3 cups) vegetable stock
1 dl (1/2 cup) white wine
1 teaspoon honey
salt and white pepper
1 tablespoon butter
1/2 red bell pepper

This dish is not just for vegetarians. Everyone will love these colorful burgers with their yellow sauce. The sauce is just as good with boiled vegetables.

PREPARATION TIME: *50 minutes*
SERVING SUGGESTION: *Serve with fried potato halves.*

BURGERS:
Mince shallot and garlic, peel and coarsely grate beets.
Simmer lentils, shallot, garlic and stock until most liquid has evaporated and mixture breaks down into a puree. Add breadcrumbs and season with salt and pepper. Form small burgers and fry on both sides in olive oil.

SAUCE:
Mince onion, garlic and yellow pepper. Sauté in olive oil with tumeric until shiny. Add stock, wine and honey and simmer 10 minutes. Pour into a food processor and puree until smooth. Strain. Season with salt and pepper. Cut red bell pepper into fine dice. Bring sauce to a boil, whisk in butter and pepper cubes.

BEVERAGE SUGGESTION: A light red wine, served lightly chilled, goes well with this dish. Try a Cabernet or Merlot from northern Italy.

Ewa Axelsson, Stenungsund

Creamy vegetable soup

SIX SERVINGS
150 g (5 oz) rutabaga
5 carrots
2 onions
1/2 leek
3 parsnips
1 jerusalem artichoke
5 potatoes
1 tablespoon butter
1 1/2 liters (6 cups) vegetable stock
1 dl (1/2 cup) crème fraiche or whipping cream
1/4 teaspoon cayenne pepper
1/4 teaspoon lemon pepper
salt

Imagine preparing this soup with your own home-grown vegetables!

PREPARATION TIME: *50 minutes*
SERVING SUGGESTION: *Serve piping hot with freshly baked bread and butter.*

Peel, clean and chop vegetables. Sauté in butter until shiny. Pour over stock and stir.
Simmer 25 minutes, until vegetables are soft. Pour into a food processor and puree until smooth. If too thick, add additional stock. Season with crème fraiche, seasonings and a little salt, if needed.

BEVERAGE SUGGESTION: The carrots add a subtle sweetness to the soup. A hearty, rather dark beer complements it well.

Cesarstugan, Östra Tunhem

BEET BURGERS WITH LENTILS AND RED-SPECKLED YELLOW PEPPER SAUCE

Wild mushroom stew

SIX – EIGHT SERVINGS
*400 g (14 oz) deer or moose meat,
in cubes*
400 g (14 oz) lean pork, in cubes
olive oil
2 large onions
4 garlic cloves
3/4 teaspoon ground paprika
50 g (1 3/4 oz) strong smoked sausage
4 dl (1 2/3 cups) sauerkraut
*1 dl (1/2 cup) dried crumbled
mushrooms or about 6 dl
(2 1/2 cups) fresh*
2 1/2 dl (1 cup) rich beef stock
2 1/2 dl (1 cup) white wine
3/4 teaspoon caraway seeds
3/4 teaspoon ground black pepper
3/4 teaspoon salt
3/4 teaspoon marjoram
3/4 teaspoon thyme
6 dl (2 1/2 cups) light cream

This dish is for the hunters of the region. The combination of Swedish game and foreign spices gives a full-bodied flavor. Hare can be substituted for deer or moose.

PREPARATION TIME: *About 90 minutes*
SERVING SUGGESTION: *Serve with boiled potatoes,
a mixed salad and pickles.*

Brown meat lightly in olive oil. Transfer to a heavy pot. Slice onion, chop garlic. Sauté until golden. Remove pan from heat and add paprika. Pour into the pot.
Cut sausage into 1 cm (1/2") cubes and add along with sauerkraut, mushrooms, stock wine and seasonings. Bring to a boil, then add cream. Cover and simmer slowly 45-60 minutes.

BEVERAGE SUGGESTION: A hearty stew demands a wine with a lot of flavor. Try one made with Syrah grapes, from the Rhône valley or from Australia (where the grape is called Shiraz).
A slightly heavier Rioja Crianza or Reserva also goes well with this dish.

Vladimir Mihalik, Skövde

Rabbit stew

SIX SERVINGS
2 rabbits, boned
butter
1-2 garlic cloves
*1-2 tablespoons grated
fresh ginger*
1 teaspoon salt
*1/2 teaspoon pepper
(preferably lemon pepper)*
*2 1/2 dl (1 cup)
whipping cream*
*1 dl (scant 1/2 cup)
orange juice concentrate*

There are few recipes for rabbit, but the meat tastes like chicken and can be prepared as such. Those who do not appreciate its slightly sweet flavor can bone it before cooking for a milder taste.

PREPARATION TIME: *About 45 minutes*
SERVING SUGGESTION: *Serve with boiled potatoes and a mixed salad.*

Brown in butter with garlic and ginger. Season with salt and pepper. Add cream and simmer several minutes. Stir in orange juice. Simmer until cooked through, about 30 minutes.

BEVERAGE SUGGESTION: This dish incorporates both sweet and sour flavors. A fresh light beer, preferably from Germany, or a dry to semi-dry white wine complement the flavors of this dish.

Elisabeth Stigen-Salén, Mellerud

WILD MUSHROOM STEW

Calves liver with pureed peas

FOUR – SIX
SERVINGS

*700 g (1 2/3 lb)
sliced calves liver
750 g (1 3/4 lb)
frozen peas
1/2 dl (3 1/2 table-
spoons) whipping
cream
1 teaspoon salt
1/2 teaspoon pepper
5 tablespoons (1/3
cup) pickled ginger
2 firm pears
1 tablespoon butter*

Many remember childhood dinners of gray liver, but now it gets a makeover. The mild flavor of calves liver come into its own when served with puree of peas and sweet and sour side dishes. No potatoes needed here!

PREPARATION TIME: *About 25 minutes*

Rinse liver and dry with paper towels.
Cook peas in lightly salted water 5 minutes.
Drain and puree in a food processor until smooth. Add cream and season. Keep warm. Just before serving, stir in butter.
Chop ginger into small dice.
Peel pears and cut into matchstick pieces.
Sauté liver in butter 3-4 minutes per side. Season.
Place liver on heated plates. Arrange a mound of pear along-side and a band of ginger over the top. Place a scoop of pureed peas alongside.

BEVERAGE SUGGESTION: This is a mild dish, and the ginger provides a sweet-sour contrast. A gentle, lightly acidic red wine with a touch of sweetness, such as a red Burgundy or a Cabernet Reserve from Bulgaria, works well here.

Gunvor Bergström, Malmö

Game stew

FOUR SERVINGS
*400 g (14 oz)
boneless moose
oil
salt and black pepper
1 onion
200 g (7 oz) fresh
chanterelles or other
wild mushrooms
3 dl (1 1/4 cups) water
2 tablespoons con-
centrated game stock
(from a jar)
8-10 crushed
juniper berries
2 carrots
1 dl (1/2 cup)
whipping cream
chopped parsley*

One advantage of making game stew is that a lovely sauce forms almost automatically after the meat has cooked a while.

PREPARATION TIME: *About 75 minutes*
SERVING SUGGESTION: *Serve with boiled potatoes
and currant jelly.*

Cube meat and brown in oil. Season with salt. Chop onions, clean and slice mushrooms.
Transfer meat to a large saucepan. Add water, stock con-centrate and juniper berries. Sauté onions and mushrooms, then add to meat.
Cover and simmer about one hour.
Cut carrots in diagonal slices and add toward the end of cooking time.
Add cream and season to taste. Sprinkle with chopped parsley.

BEVERAGE SUGGESTION: A hearty red wine is best with game stew. Chose one with well-developed fruitiness, such as a Cabernet Sauvignon from Chile or Australia.

Rikard Johansson, Skövde

CALVES LIVER WITH PUREED PEAS

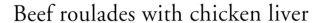

Beef roulades with chicken liver

THE COOKBOOK
CONTEST
SECOND PRIZE
INDIVIDUAL DISHES

EIGHT SERVINGS
400 g (14 oz) chicken livers
1/4 teaspoon chile powder
1/4 teaspoon curry powder
1 teaspoon salt
8 bacon slices
16 slices Swiss cheese
1 dl (1/2 cup) raisins
16 thin slices
top round steak
2 tablespoons butter
6 dl (2 1/2 cups) beef stock
4 tablespoons (1/4 cup)
instant blending flour
2 dl (3/4 cup)
whipping cream

This is a traditional Swedish Sunday dinner dish,
but with a surprise inside.

PREPARATION TIME: *About 40 minutes*
SERVING SUGGESTION: *Serve with baked potato
halves.*

Clean livers, removing any veins and green parts.
Combine chile, curry and salt and sprinkle over liver.
Place a piece of liver, half a slice of bacon, a slice
of cheese and a few raisins on each piece of meat.
Roll up and fasten edges with toothpicks.
Brown roulades in butter in a large skillet.
Add stock, cover and simmer over low heat about
30 minutes.
Remove roulades from pan and discard toothpicks.
Whisk flour into a few tablespoons of the cream.
Bring stock and remaining cream to a boil. Whisk
in flour-cream mixture and simmer until thickened.
Season to taste.

BEVERAGE SUGGESTION: A medium-bodied red wine
with moderate tannin, such as Beaujolais, Valpolicella, or
one from the south of France works well here. Thanks to
the curry and bacon, a full-flavored dry white wine goes
equally well.

Lars Gillis Larsson, Gothenburg

Root vegetable cake with salt pork

FOUR – SIX
SERVINGS

400 g (14 oz) potatoes
300 g (10 oz) carrots
100 g (3 1/2 oz)
kohlrabi
100 g (3 1/2 oz) radish
2 garlic cloves
1 onion
2 eggs
1 dl (1/2 cup)
whipping cream
salt and pepper
2 dl (1 cup) grated
Swiss cheese
400 – 500 g salted
pork shoulder

Salt pork with root vegetables is a classic Swedish
rustic dish. A lot of time is saved since the vegetables
are finely shredded and need no supervision during
cooking.

PREPARATION TIME: *About one hour*
OVEN TEMPERATURE: *200 °C (400 °F)*
SERVING SUGGESTION: *Serve with iceberg lettuce,
tomatoes and cucumber.*

Peel vegetables and grate in a food processor.
Combine vegetables and arrange in an ovenproof dish.
Whisk egg, cream, salt and pepper and pour over
vegetables. Sprinkle with grated cheese.
Bake 30-40 minutes on center oven shelf, until
vegetables are soft and cake is golden brown.
This mixture also can be made into burgers and fried.
Cut pork into shreds and fry over medium heat
without added fat.

Lisette Klingström and Erika Magnusson, Skövde

Beef stew with currants

SIX SERVINGS
1 kg (2 1/4 lb) boneless
beef, preferably chuck
1 dl (1/2 cup) black
currant juice concentrate
4 dl (1 2/3 cups) water
1 beef bouillon cube
1/2 teaspoon salt
1/4 teaspoon black pepper
1 bay leaf
1 teaspoon thyme
12 pearl onions
1 1/2 tablespoons flour
1/2 dl (3 1/2 tablespoons)
water

A similar stew bears the name of Carnegie, then Hiram, a well-known food-writer, called it a Porter steak. Now this dish has been modernized with black currant juice. This stew tastes best the day after it is made.

PREPARATION TIME: *45 minutes*
SERVING SUGGESTION: *Serve with boiled potatoes and vegetables.*

Cut meat into chunks.
Bring juice concentrate and water to a boil and add bouillon cube.
Add meat, a few pieces at a time, so the liquid stays boiling. Add salt, pepper and herbs, and simmer 35 minutes. Peel onions and add, then simmer 10 minutes more. Whisk flour into water and add. Simmer 5 minutes.

Christina Asplund, Gothenburg

Orange-glazed ham

FOUR SERVINGS
1 kg (2 1/4 lb) fresh ham
2 teaspoons butter
1 teaspoon salt
1/2 teaspoon white pepper
Marinade/glaze:
2 1/2 dl (1 cup) fresh orange juice
2 1/2 tablespoons honey
3 shallots, chopped
1 tablespoon chopped fresh mint
1/2 teaspoon ground coriander
Garnish:
1 orange
20 g (2 tablespoons) sliced almonds, toasted
Sauce:
2 dl (3/4 cup) cooking liquid from ham
2 dl (3/4 cup) beef or chicken stock
2 teaspoons cornstarch stirred into 1 tablespoon cold water
3 tablespoons port wine

Pork and citrus fruits are a successful combination. The hearty flavor of the meat is tempered by the acidity of the fruit. In this recipe, a traditional pork roast is modernized with oranges sliced almonds.

PREPARATION TIME: *About one hour*
OVEN TEMPERATURE: *175°C (350°F)*
SERVING SUGGESTION: *Serve with hasselback potatoes and vegetables.*

Brown ham in butter. Transfer to an ovenproof dish and sprinkle with salt and pepper.
Combine marinade in a saucepan and simmer, uncovered, 5 minutes. Pour marinade over meat. Insert a meat thermometer. Roast until internal temperature reaches 70°C (160°F), about 45 minutes. Baste a few times during roasting.
Let meat rest about 20 minutes before slicing. Cut into thin slices and arrange on a serving platter. Peel and slice orange. There should be no membrane adhering to slices. Arrange on meat. Sprinkle with toasted almond slices.

SAUCE:
Strain cooking juices. There should be about 2 dl (3/4 cup). Combine with stock and bring to a boil. Thicken with cornstarch mixture. Stir in port wine. Correct seasoning.

BEVERAGE SUGGESTION: Forget the rule about red wine and meat – pork often tastes better with white wine! An aromatic white wine complements this sweet-sour dish. Serve with a white wine from Alsace, Germany or the Rhône valley.

Christina Asplund, Gothenburg

BEEF STEW WITH CURRANTS

Filet of lamb with herbed potatoes and stuffed tomatoes

FOUR SERVINGS
Herb crust:
100 g (3 1/2 oz) melted butter
1 garlic clove
2 tablespoons chopped fresh parsley
2 tablespoons chopped fresh basil
2 tablespoons chopped fresh thyme
2 tablespoons chopped fresh rosemary
1 dl (1/2 cup) fresh white breadcrumbs
1 dl (1/2 cup) grated Swiss cheese

Herbed potatoes:
700 g (1 1/2 lb) winter potatoes
2 tablespoons pesto sauce (from a jar)
salt and pepper

Tomatoes:
4 medium plum tomatoes
1 onion
1 garlic clove
olive oil
150 g (5 oz) ricotta cheese
50 g (2 oz) chevre (white goat cheese)
1 teaspoon dried rosemary, crushed

Sauce:
1 onion
2 garlic cloves
needles from 3 rosemary branches
1 tablespoon butter
4 dl (1 2/3 cups) whipping cream
salt and pepper
1 dl (1/2 cup) lamb or chicken stock

600 g (1 1/3 lbs) skinless and boneless loin of lamb
olive oil

This time-consuming dish is worth the effort. Lamb works well with pesto and chevre, and the result is a festive main dish.

PREPARATION TIME: *Day 1: about 40 minutes; day 2: about 50 minutes*
OVEN TEMPERATURE: *180°C (350°F)*

DAY 1:
Combine butter, garlic and herbs in a blender or food processor, then add bread and cheese. Refrigerate.
Peel and cube potatoes. Boil until soft, drain and divide into two equal parts. While still hot, mash one with pesto until light green and smooth. Fold in remaining potato cubes. Season with salt and pepper. Refrigerate.

DAY 2:
Cut off tomato tops, then spoon out seeds and flesh.
Chop onion and garlic, and sauté in olive oil until soft.
Mash cheeses, then stir in sautéed onions and rosemary. Stuff tomatoes with this mixture.

SAUCE:
Chop onions, garlic and rosemary, and sauté in butter. Add cream and bring to a boil. Simmer about 10 minutes. Season with salt, pepper and stock. Pour into a blender and blend until smooth.

BEFORE SERVING:
Divide meat into four pieces of equal size. Brown lightly in olive oil. Transfer to an oven pan. Top with herb butter. Make four mounds of potatoes and place tomatoes alongside. Roast until meat is done and tomatoes are soft, about 10 minutes.

BEVERAGE SUGGESTION: The most natural choice of beverage for this Provençale-inspired dish is a delicate and fruity red wine from the same area.

Ulrik Lindelöv, Gothenburg

Deviled burgers

FOUR SERVINGS
*400 g (14 oz) ground pork or
meatloaf mixture
1 egg
1 medium boiled potato, grated
1 teaspoon salt
1/4 teaspoon pepper
1 dl (1/3 cup) milk or beef stock
1/2 small onion
2 tablespoons grated
horseradish
1 tablespoon Dijon-style
mustard
corn oil*

*Sauce:
6 dl (2 1/2 cups) beef stock
4 tablespoons (1/4 cup)
instant blending flour
2 dl (3/4 cup) whipping cream*

These deviled burgers are a pleasant change from the
traditional variety. Horseradish and mustard add a piquant
touch.

PREPARATION TIME: *45 minutes*
SERVING SUGGESTION: *Serve with boiled potatoes, vegetables
and currant jelly.*

Combine ground meat with egg, potato, salt and pepper.
Gradually add milk to make a fluffy mixture. Divide into
four flat burgers.
Mince onion. Combine with horseradish and mustard.
Place a spoonful of this mixture on each burger. Fold
together, enclosing filling, and flatten. Press edges well.
Fry in oil over medium heat about 3 minutes per side.

SAUCE:
Bring stock to a boil. Whisk flour into cream and add.
Simmer until thickened.

Anna Berg, Åsarp

Quick smoked pork stew

FOUR SERVINGS
400 g (14 oz) Canadian bacon,
without rind, in one piece
1 garlic clove
1 medium leek
1 red bell pepper
1 green bell pepper
2 dl (3/4 cup) whipping cream
2 dl (3/4 cup) crème fraiche or more
whipping cream
5 tablespoons (1/3 cup) tomato paste
2 teaspoons curry powder
salt and pepper

An easy and popular dish

PREPARATION TIME: *About 30 minutes*
SERVING SUGGESTION: *Serve with rice and a salad.*

Cut meat into strips. Chop garlic. Clean and slice leek. Combine cream and cream fraiche in a large saucepan and bring to a boil. Add remaining ingedients. Simmer 10 minutes over low heat. If using only whipping cream, it may be necessary to thicken with 2 teaspoons corn-starch stirred into 1 tablespoon cold water.

BEVERAGE SUGGESTION: This everyday dish is good enough to serve on special occasions. Serve with a semi-dry white wine made with Riesling grapes. Their light sweetness and fresh acidity balance the salty character of the pork.

Marinett Hidendahl, Östra Frölunda

Mushroom-stuffed noisettes of roe deer

FOUR SERVINGS
Noisettes:
1 tablespoon minced onion
5 dl (2 cups) wild mushrooms
butter
1/2 teaspoon salt
1/2 teaspoon white pepper
4 roe deer loin slices, about 100 g
(3 1/2 oz) each

Root vegetables:
50 g (2 oz) celeriac
50 g (2 oz) rutabaga
1 medium carrot
1 small leek
2 tablespoons butter
1/4 teaspoon thyme
1/2 teaspoon salt
1/2 teaspoon white pepper

Lingonberry sauce:
3 dl (1 1/4 cups) game stock
1/2 dl (3 1/2 tablespoons) lingonberries
1 tablespoon crushed juniper berries
1 dl (1/2 cup) whipping cream

Potato pancakes:
3 dl (1 1/4 cups) grated potatoes
2 eggs
1/2 dl (3 1/2 tablespoons) flour
1/2 teaspoon salt
1/2 teaspoon white pepper
butter

A noisette is really a thin piece of meat, but in this case, the slices need to be 2-3 cm thick to hold the filling. If fresh mushrooms are unavailable, use canned.

PREPARATION TIME: *About one hour*
SERVING SUGGESTION: *Serve with fresh lingonberries and garnish with parsley.*

Sauté onion and mushrooms in butter until liquid has evaporated and mushrooms begin to sizzle. Season with salt and pepper. Chop in a food processor.
Cut a pocket in each slice of deer and fill with mushroom mixture. Fasten with a toothpick. Sauté meat in butter about 5 minutes per side. Season with salt and pepper.

ROOT VEGETABLES:
Shred vegetables and sauté in butter about 5 minutes. Season with thyme, salt and pepper.

LINGONBERRY SAUCE:
Reduce stock and berries over high heat about 5 minutes. Whisk in cream.

POTATO PANCAKES:
Combine shredded potato, eggs, flour and seasonings. Fry in butter until golden, about 5 minutes per side. Makes 8 pancakes.

Karen Pilgaard, Tibro

The best meatballs in Sweden

SIX SERVINGS
3/4 dl (1/3 cup) rolled oats
1 tablespoon potato starch
2 tablespoons veal stock
concentrate (from a jar)
1 dl (scant 1/2 cup) water
1 egg
1 tablespoon grated onion
1 teaspoon salt
1/2 teaspoon ground
white pepper
butter

Sauce:
3 dl (1 1/4 cups) pan juices
1 beef bouillon cube
2 tablespoons flour
1 dl (1/3 cup) milk or water
1 teaspoon soy sauce
3 tablespoons whipping
cream (optional)

Oats are an old-fashioned filler for ground meat dishes. They blend easily with the meat and add a little flavor.

PREPARATION TIME: *About 40 minutes*
SERVING SUGGESTION: *Serve with boiled potatoes, vegetables and lingonberries.*

Combine oats, potato starch, stock concentrate and water. Let soak 10 minutes.
Add egg, onion, salt and pepper. Add ground meat and mix well.
Form into meatballs with oiled hands.
Brown meatballs in butter 5-6 minutes. Shake the pan to keep them round. Transfer to a serving dish and keep warm.

SAUCE:
Deglaze pan with warm water and pour into a saucepan. There should be about 3 dl (1 1/4 cups). Crush bouillon cube and add. Whisk flour into milk and add, whisking constantly. Simmer 3-5 minutes. Season with soy sauce and cream, if desired.

Christina Asplund, Gothenburg

Dill-marinated pork loin

FOUR – SIX SERVINGS
Marinade:
2 dl (3/4 cup) apple juice
2 tablespoons soy sauce
1 tablespoon oil
1 dl (1/3 cup) chopped dill
1 teaspoon dried rosemary
1 teaspoon dried tarragon

1 kg (2 1/4 lb) boneless
loin of pork
1 teaspoon salt
1/2 teaspoon pepper

Veal with dill sauce is a traditional Swedish dish. This recipe uses boneless pork instead.

PREPARATION TIME: *About 1 hour plus at least 6 hours for marinating*
OVEN TEMPERATURE: *175°C (350°F)*
SERVING SUGGESTION: *Serve with boiled potatoes, a green salad and a cold sour cream sauce with lots of chopped fresh dill.*

Combine ingredients for marinade in a heavy plastic bag and add meat. Seal bag and marinate at least 6 hours in the refrigerator. Transfer meat to an oven tray and sprinkle with salt and pepper. Insert a meat thermometer. Roast until internal temperature reaches 70°C (160°F), about 50 minutes. Remove and let rest at least 10 minutes before serving.

BEVERAGE SUGGESTION: The acidity of the marinade complicates the choice of wine. A light bitter beer is best.

Christina Asplund, Gothenburg

Bacon-wrapped pork tenderloin with parsleyed carrots and green hollandaise

FOUR SERVINGS
Pork tenderloin:
600 g (1 1/3 lb) pork tenderloin
3 tablespoons hazelnuts
2 tablespoons breadcrumbs
2 tablespoons minced onion
1/2 teaspoon salt
1/4 teaspoon ground
black pepper
8 bacon slices
4 tablespoons (1/4 cup) butter

Carrots:
300 g (10 oz) carrots
2 tablespoons butter
1 tablespoon chopped parsley

Green hollandaise:
1/2 onion
a few stalks parsley
5-6 white peppercorns, crushed
1/2 dl (3 1/2 tablespoons) water
150 g (5 oz) unsalted butter
3 egg yolks
3-4 tablespoons chopped chives
juice of 1/2 lemon
salt

Pork tenderloin and bacon are a good match.

PREPARATION TIME: *80 minutes*
SERVING SUGGESTION: *Serve with new potatoes rolled in chopped dill.*

Remove all membrane from pork tenderloin and cut into 8 pieces of equal size. Mix hazelnuts and crumbs in a blender. Add onion and seasonings.
Wrap each piece of tenderloin in a bacon slice, then dip cut surfaces of pork into the breadcrumb mixture. Fry in butter about 5 minutes per side.
Wash or scrape carrots and slice into coins. Boil in lightly salted water about 5 minutes. Drain. Melt butter, add carrots and parsley. Season if necessary.

SAUCE:
Chop onion and parsley and place in a saucepan with peppercorns and water. Bring to a boil. Strain and reserve. Melt butter. Whisk egg yolks with liquid in a double boiler. Whisk in butter in a thin stream. The butter and eggs should be the same temperature. Season with chives, lemon juice and salt.

BEVERAGE SUGGESTION: This dish, with its rich sauce, is flavorful yet mild and needs a wine with a certain amount of freshness. A light red wine, such as a Gamay from the south of France, or a dry white wine go well with this dish.

Karen Pilgaard, Tibro

Lamb stew

FOUR SERVINGS
4 onions
1-2 garlic cloves
olive oil
750 g (1 3/4 lb) boneless lamb stew meat
8 fresh tomatoes, peeled or
1 can whole peeled tomatoes
1 teaspoon salt
1/2 teaspoon ground
black pepper
1 teaspoon thyme
2-3 dl (1 cup) lamb or beef stock
1/2 dl (3 1/2 tablespoons) chopped parsley
1/2 dl (3 1/2 tablespoons) chopped chives
1 tablespoon flour
1 dl (1/3 cup) crème fraiche or whipping cream

An easy-to-make stew, which even lamb skeptics will enjoy. Onions and tomatoes hide the characteristic lamb flavor somewhat.

PREPARATION TIME: *About one hour*
SERVING SUGGESTION: *Serve with boiled or riced potatoes and a green salad.*

Chop onions and garlic. Brown with lamb in olive oil. Add tomatoes, salt, pepper and thyme. Add stock and simmer until meat is tender, about 45 minutes. Stir in parsley and chives. Whisk flour into crème fraiche and add. Bring to a boil and simmer until thickened.

BEVERAGE SUGGESTION: Lamb, especially when paired with garlic and tomato, is perfect with a cask-aged Spanish red wine, preferably a Rioja or a wine from Ribera del Duero.

Susanna Kindberg-Laakso, Ulricehamn

BACON-WRAPPED PORK TENDERLOIN WITH PARSLEYED CARROTS AND GREEN HOLLANDAISE

Cherry-baked apples

FOUR SERVINGS
3 1/2 dl (1 1/2 cups) water
3 1/2 dl (1 1/2 cups) sugar
*2 tablespoons vanilla sugar
(or 1 vanilla bean, split)*
4 large apples
2 tablespoons melted butter
2 tablespoons corn syrup

Filling:
*8 milk biscuits or
shortbread cookies*
*75 g (2 3/4 oz) semi-sweet
chocolate*
*1 1/2 dl (2/3 cup) pitted
cherries, halved*

Sauce
2 1/2 dl (1 cup) milk
2 tablespoons vanilla sugar
2 tablespoons sugar
4 egg yolk

A completely new filling for baked apples.
Try substituting other chopped fruit or berries. It tastes
good with cold custard, too.

PREPARATION TIME: *30 minutes*
OVEN TEMPERATURE: *175°C (350°F)*
Bring water, sugar and vanilla sugar to a boil.
Simmer 2 minutes. If using vanilla bean, remove and
reserve for sauce. Pour into an ovenproof dish.
Peel and core apples. Brush all over and inside with
melted butter and syrup.
Crush cookies and chop chocolate. Combine with
cherries and stuff into apples.
Transfer apples to ovenproof dish. Bake about 20 minutes
or until soft.

SAUCE:
Scald milk. Whisk sugars with egg yolks until light
and lemon-colored. Whisk into milk. Heat, whisking
constantly, over low heat until thickened.
Pour sauce over apples and serve.

Cissi Lehtinen, Grästorp

Summer strawberry dessert

Years ago, stale and broken cookies were
used instead of sponge cake. The dessert
was called "angel food" and was every
child's favorite.

PREPARATION TIME: *About 15 minutes for
preserves, plus 15 minutes, plus about
3 hours for the dessert to set.*

Place 1 tablespoon preserves in the
bottom of four dessert dishes. Top with
sponge cake. Then divide remaining
preserves among the four dishes. Let set
until cake is soft and juicy. If should be
completely soaked with fresh strawberry
preserves.
Whip cream until it clots. Pipe over
desserts and sprinkle with chopped
almonds.
Raspberries can also be used in this dessert.

Margareta Wassenius, Uddevalla

FOUR SERVINGS
*6 dl (2 1/2 cups) fresh strawberry preserves
(made by stirring together 3 parts fruit to
2 parts sugar)*
*4 slices sponge cake, 5 cm (2") square and
2 cm (3/4") thick*
1 1/2 dl (2/3 cup) whipping cream
10 almonds, chopped

Gooseberry gazpacho with cardamom ice cream

FOUR SERVINGS
Gazpacho:
1 1/2 liters (6 cups)
gooseberries
1/2 dl (3 1/2 table-
spoons) coarsely
chopped fresh mint
2 dl (3/4 cup)
white wine
2 dl (3/4 cup) fresh
orange juice
1 1/2 dl (2/3 cup) sugar

Ice cream:
4 tablespoons (1/4
cup) cardamom pods
5 dl (2 cups)
light cream
4 egg yolks
1 1/2 dl (2/3 cup) sugar
2 tablespoons Grand
Marnier

Gooseberries and cardamom are an unusual flavor combination. For a similar, yet easier dessert, sprinkle ground cardamom over vanilla ice cream and serve with warm gooseberry sauce.

PREPARATION TIME: *One hour, plus 30 minutes in an ice cream machine or 3 hours in a freezer*

GAZPACHO:
Combine berries, mint, wine, juice and sugar in a saucepan. Split vanilla bean, scrape out seeds and add, reserving bean for another use. Bring to a boil. Simmer 5 minutes. Remove from heat and let rest 1 hour.
Puree in a food processor, then strain.

ICE CREAM:
Crush cardamom pods in a mortar to extract seeds. Discard pods. Bring milk, cream and cardamom to a boil. Cool 30 minutes. Strain.
Whisk egg yolks and sugar over low heat until thickened. Whisk in milk mixture. Cool, then stir in liqueur.
Freeze in an ice cream machine or pour into a mold and freeze, stirring several times during freezing process.
Pour gazpacho into bowls. Top with a scoop of ice cream.

Eliasson family, Gothenburg

Cherry baked Alaska

SIX – EIGHT
SERVINGS
Base:
2 dl (3/4 cup)
milk biscuit
crumbs
50 g (3 table-
spoons) melted
butter

Filling:
400 g (14 oz)
cherry-flavored
cheese
1 1/2 tablespoons
cherry liqueur
2 1/2 dl (1 cup)
whipping cream

Meringue:
3 egg whites
1 1/2 dl (2/3 cup)
sugar

This is a good dessert to have in the freezer when unexpected guests arrive. Just beat the meringue and bake. If cherry-flavored cheese is unavailable, blend chopped cherries into light cream cheese.

PREPARATION TIME: *30 minutes plus 4 hours in the freezer*
OVEN TEMPERATURE: *200°C (400°) for base and 250°C (475°F) for meringue*

Combine crumbs and butter. Press into the bottom of an ovenproof dish. Bake on center oven shelf about 5 minutes.
Beat cheese with liqueur until light and fluffy. Whip cream and fold into cheese mixture. Spread over baked crumb base. Freeze.
Just before serving, beat egg whites until soft peaks form. Add sugar and beat until very stiff. Spread over frozen cake and bake about 5 minutes, until meringue turns light beige.

Margareta Bengtsson and Anna Rehnstedt, Falköping

GOOSEBERRY GAZPACHO WITH CARDAMOM ICE CREAM

Minted pear tartlet with blueberry sorbet

FOUR SERVINGS
Blueberry sorbet:
4 dl (1 2/3 cups) blueberries
1 tablespoon sugar
2 tablespoons cherry liqueur
3 egg whites
3 tablespoons sugar

2 large pears
2 tablespoons mint jelly
1 1/2 dl (2/3 cup) crème fraiche
or dairy sour cream

Pears and blueberries are fine local products. They are every bit as good as all the imported exotic fruits available year-round. Custard cups can be used instead of tartlet pans.

PREPARATION TIME: *: One hour plus one hour for marinating and 30 minutes in an ice cream machine*

SORBET:
Mash 1 dl (1/2 cup) of the blueberries and mix with sugar and liqueur. Refrigerate one hour.
Simmer remaining blueberries with a little water about 5 minutes. Drain and place in a food processor with marinated berries. Puree until smooth. Strain.
Beat egg whites until soft peaks form. Add sugar and beat until almost stiff. Fold in pureed blueberries.
Freeze in an ice cream machine or pour into a mold and freeze, stirring several times during the freezing process.

Peel, core and slice pears. Beat mint jelly into crème fraiche. Layer pears and crème fraiche mixture in tartlet shells. Bake about 15 minutes. Cool slightly before serving with sorbet.

Janne Hedman, Lundsbrunn

Apple roll

12 PIECES
Base:
75 g (2 3/4 oz) unsalted butter
1 dl (scant 1/2 cup) sugar
4 egg yolks
2-3 tablespoons milk
1 1/2 dl (2/3 cup) flour
1 1/2 teaspoons baking powder
4 egg whites
2 dl (3/4 cup) sugar
50 g (1 3/4 oz) sliced almonds

Filling
2 dl (3/4 cup) whipping cream
2 apples
1-3 tablespoons Swedish
punsch liqueur

Garnish:
confectioner's sugar
lemon balm

A cake roll can be served as a dessert or with coffee. This punsch-flavored apple roll is a perfect example.

PREPARATION TIME: *About one hour*
OVEN TEMPERATURE: *150 °C (300 °F)*

BASE:
Line a 25x35 cm (10x14") pan with baking parchment .
Beat butter and sugar until light and fluffy. Add egg yolks, one at a time. Add milk, then flour and baking powder. Beat until smooth.
In a large clean bowl, beat egg whites until foamy, then add half the sugar. Beat until soft peaks form, then add remaining sugar and beat until stiff.
Spread base mixture into pan. Top with meringue. Sprinkle with almonds.
Bake on lowest oven shelf about 25 minutes.
Remove cake from pan and cool slightly. Remove paper from cake and loosely roll up lengthwise.
Whip cream. Peel and grate apples. Mix apples and whipped cream (so they won't turn brown). Stir in punsch.
Unroll cake and spread with apple filling. Roll up.
Place on a serving dish and sprinkle with confectioner's sugar. Garnish with lemon balm.

Christina Asplund, Gothenburg

MINTED PEAR TARTLET WITH BLUEBERRY SORBET

Lemon-basil curd with almond praline

FOUR SERVINGS
Tuiles:
100 g (3 1/2 oz) almonds
100 g (3 1/2 oz) unsalted butter
100 g (1/2 cup) sugar
1 tablespoon flour
1 tablespoon grated lemon rind

Curd:
1 gelatin sheet
juice of 1 lemon
75 g (2 3/4 oz) unsalted butter
1/2 dl (3 1/2 tablespoons) sugar
4 egg yolks
1/2 dl (3 1/2 tablespoons) chopped basil

Praline:
1/2 dl (3 1/2 tablespoons) sugar
30 g (1/2 cup) sliced almonds

This is a variation on lemon curd and can be used as a tart filling or as a spread for bread. It's very rich, to be enjoyed in small portions.

PREPARATION TIME: *25 minutes plus one hour in the refrigerator*
OVEN TEMPERATURE: *200 °C (400 °F)*
SERVING SUGGESTION: *Serve with fresh berries, basil leaves and spun sugar.*

Grind half the almonds and chop the rest. Combine all ingredients in a saucepan and melt over low heat. Place teaspoonfuls of mixture far apart (to allow for spreading during baking) on a greased cookie sheet. Bake until golden, about 5 minutes. Cool slightly. Drape over a rolling pin, if desired.
Soak gelatin in cold water to soften, about 5 minutes. Simmer lemon juice, butter, sugar and egg yolks over low heat until thickened, whisking constantly. Squeeze excess water from gelatin sheet and add with basil. Simmer until dissolved. Pour curd into four small custard cups. Bake 10 minutes. Refrigerate at least one hour before serving.
Melt sugar in a skillet. When light brown, add almonds, stirring well. Pour onto a lightly oiled metal cookie sheet to stiffen. Chop into small pieces. Sprinkle on individual plates. Unmold curds and place in the center. Garnish with tuiles.

Håkan Thörnström, Gothenburg

Lingonberry bavarian cream

FOUR SERVINGS
1 tablespoon powdered gelatin
1/2 dl (3 1/2 tablespoons) water
2 eggs
3 tablespoons sugar
1 teaspoon vanilla sugar (or 1/2 teaspoon vanilla extract)
4 dl (1 2/3 cups) natural yogurt
1 dl (1/2cup) lingon-berry preserves
1 dl (1/2 cup) whipping cream
fresh or frozen lingonberries

This bavarian cream is a fresh-flavored dessert.

PREPARATION TIME: *30 minutes plus 3 hours in the refrigerator*

Sprinkle gelatin over water to soften, about 5 minutes. Melt over low heat.
Separate eggs. Beat egg yolks and sugar until light and lemon-colored.
Beat vanilla sugar and yogurt into egg mixture. Add gelatin in a thin stream, beating constantly. Add lingon-berry preserves. Whip cream and fold into lingonberry mixture.
Beat egg whites until stiff and fold into lingonberry mixture. Pour into a mold. Refrigerate 2-3 hours. To serve, dip mold into hot water a few seconds, then unmold. Garnish with lingonberries.

Lena Rydberg and Sandra Loft Svensson, Mariestad

LEMON-BASIL CURD WITH ALMOND PRALINE

White chocolate and passion fruit mousse

FOUR SERVINGS
2 egg yolks
2 tablespoons sugar
1 tablespoon white wine
1 gelatin sheet
130 g (4 1/2 oz) white chocolate
2-3 tablespoons passion fruit puree (strained passion fruit flesh)
2 dl (3/4 cup) whipping cream

White chocolate contains no cocoa at all. It is made from cocoa butter, sugar, powdered milk, vanilla and lecithin. White chocolate is very decorative with exotic fruits and is excellent in desserts.

PREPARATION TIME: *15 minutes plus at least one hour in the refrigerator*
SERVING SUGGESTION: *Serve with any of the following: Chocolate sauce, fresh red berries, exotic fruit, lemon balm, spun sugar, chocolate cigars.*

Whisk together egg yolks, sugar and white wine in a double boiler until thick.
Soak gelatin sheet in cold water to soften, about 5 minutes. Squeeze excess water from gelatin and melt in warm egg yolk mixture. Chop chocolate and add. Stir in passion fruit puree. Cool to room temperature.
Whip cream and carefully fold into chocolate mixture. Refrigerate at least one hour before serving. Form eggs of mousse with a warm spoon.

Håkan Thörnström, Gothenburg

Rhubarb marzipan compote in a filo packet

FOUR SERVINGS
Marzipan:
2 cold boiled potatoes
200 g (7 oz) almond paste
100 g (3 1/2 oz) unsalted butter, softened
2 egg yolks
1 tablespoon potato starch

Compote:
5 dl (2 cups) chopped rhubarb
100 g (1 cup) strawberries
2 tablespoons strawberry juice
2 tablespoons water
1 teaspoon potato starch stirred into 1 tablespoon water

8 sheets filo pastry, 20x15 cm (8x6") each
melted butter

This is a dessert for someone who loves to cook and who appreciates the interaction of almonds, strawberries and rhubarb. It tastes wonderful with homemade custard flavored with real vanilla, but it is also good with vanilla ice cream.

PREPARATION TIME: *About one hour*
OVEN TEMPERATURE: *160°C (320°F)*
SERVING SUGGESTION: *Serve with vanilla custard.*

MARZIPAN:
In a large bowl, mash cold potatoes. Coarsely grate almond paste and add with remaining ingredients. Beat until smooth.

COMPOTE:
Place rhubarb in a saucepan. Add strawberries, juice and water. Halve strawberries if large. Bring to a boil and thicken with potato starch mixture. Cool.

PACKETS:
Layer two sheets of filo, brushing with butter in between. Repeat three times.
Place a spoonful of compote in the middle of the pastry. Twist into a bundle.
Bake 20 minutes.

Ulrik Lindelöv, Gothenburg

WHITE CHOCOLATE AND PASSION FRUIT MOUSSE

Almond cream torte with blueberry compote

12 – 15 PIECES
Cake layers:
1 1/2 dl (2/3 cup) almonds
1 1/2 dl (2/3 cup) sugar
4 egg whites

Praline:
3/4 dl (1/3) cup sugar
20 almonds, chopped

Pastry cream:
4 egg yolks
2 dl (3/4 cup)
whipping cream
1 dl (1/3 cup) sugar
50 g (3 tablespoons)
unsalted butter

Blueberry compote:
100 g (1 cup) frozen
blueberries
75 g (3/8 cup) sugar
1 teaspoon cornstarch
stirred into
1 tablespoon cold water

Almond buttercream torte is the oldest kind of torte found in Swedish cookbooks. It is just as popular today as it was 200 years ago. It is also called Zuleika torte, success torte, Oscar II's torte and Säby torte, but the latter is made with chocolate buttercream. Sometimes, it's decorated with sliced almonds or toasted nuts, sometimes with crushed praline, and for Easter, it is garnished with marzipan chicks. Now, pastry cream is often substituted for buttercream.

PREPARATION TIME: *One hour*
OVEN TEMPERATURE: *200°C (400°F)*
SERVING SUGGESTION: *Serve with any of the following: Blueberry compote, strawberry sauce, lemon balm and spun sugar.*

CAKE LAYERS:
Draw two circles, about 24 cm (10") in diameter, on baking parchment. Grease and flour lightly. Place on a cookie sheet.
Blanch almonds and grind, preferably by hand.
Combine with sugar.
Beat egg whites until stiff, then fold almond mixture gently into egg whites.
Spread cake mixture into the circles on the paper.
Bake 15 minutes.
Remove paper and cool.

PRALINE:
Melt sugar with chopped almonds in a skillet. Pour onto a greased cookie sheet and cool. Crush into small bits.

PASTRY CREAM:
Combine egg yolks, cream, sugar and butter in stainless steel saucepan. Heat carefully, whisking constantly, until thick. (If it curdles, add a little boiling water). Cool.

BLUEBERRY COMPOTE:
Simmer blueberries and sugar in a saucepan.
Add cornstarch mixture and boil until thickened. Simmer 3 minutes. Cool slightly before serving.

TO ASSEMBLE:
Stir praline into pastry cream. Spread half of pastry cream onto one cake layer. Top with other layer and spread with remaining cream. Garnish with blueberry compote and fresh berries.

Håkan Thörnström, Gothenburg

ALMOND CREAM TORTE WITH BLUEBERRY COMPOTE

A coffee party with
seven kinds of baked goods

EACH GENERATION HAS its own picture of how a coffee party should look.

The elderly think of a table covered with a hand-embroidered cloth and set with fine china and a shiny, newly polished silver coffeepot. In this case, seven kinds of pastry would be an understatement. Any respectable coffee table would have to feature at least ten kinds of baked goods, including two sweet yeast breads, assorted cookies and biscuits and a whipped cream cake. And to go with the cake, a liqueur served in sparkling crystal glasses.

THE NEXT GENERATION, grown up with the idea that "time is money" and notions of "wasted womanpower", may instead offer tea, assorted biscuits, and a cheese board. A tall glass of beer and simple sandwiches also can take the place of a traditional coffee table. The most important thing is to be sociable in an easy, relaxing way.

TODAY'S YOUNG FAMILIES often celebrate birthdays with coffee parties, but with a cake buffet rather than cookies and sweet breads. Today's table is set with ice cream cakes, American cheesecake, French chocolate cakes, fruit pies and other sweets. The traditional marzipan-covered "princess torte" – these days taking the shape of a horse's head, guitar, or whatever the guest of honor prefers – is almost always included. Liqueur is perhaps exchanged for a glass of misty porter. A warm summer day in the garden is the perfect setting for a cake buffet.

THE POPULAR COOKBOOK, *Seven Kinds of Cookies and Cakes,* was first published in 1945 and was an immediate success. And new editions still appear every few years. Many a coffee party has been prepared exclusively from recipes in this book. Some of the most typical and popular recipes include various kinds of Danish pastry, sweet rusks, sweet breads, Tosca cake, coconut cakes, vanilla crescents, sugar rings, Finnish sticks, oatmeal snaps, chocolate slices and many many more. A smart housewife made a large batch of sugar cookie dough, which she flavored in different ways and baked in different shapes.

The whipped cream cake is probably Sweden's favorite cake today. For many, it is a real summer treat, with its light sponge base and filling of vanilla cream and berries or mashed fruit. Whipped cream is lavishly piped all over and the biggest and loveliest strawberries or raspberries are carefully placed on top. In America, it's called a Swedish Cake.

The coffee party
"The hostess receives her guests in the sitting-room, whether the coffee table is laid there or in the dining-room. If the coffee table is in the sitting-room, however, one is not supposed to sit down at it, but in another part of the room. Many do not sit down at all; they remain standing, awaiting the moment when everyone has arrived and the coffee is brought in."

FROM "THE HOUSEWIFE'S LIBRARY", 1935

Ring cookies

PREPARATION TIME: *About 2 hours*
OVEN TEMPERATURE: *175°C (350°F)*

YIELD: ABOUT 40 COOKIES
1 1/2 dl (2/3 cup) whipping cream
1 dl (scant 1/4 cup) water
25 g (1 oz) fresh yeast
about 5 dl (2 cups) flour
200 g (7 oz) unsalted butter, softenened
pearl sugar or crushed
sugar cubes

Combine cream and water.
Crumble in yeast. Stir.
Gradually add flour. Knead
dough a few minutes, cover, and let rise
until doubled.
Knead in butter, adding more flour if
necessary. Roll the dough into finger-thick
lengths and form into rings, about 5 cm (2")
in diameter.
Dip in pearl sugar and place on a cookie
sheet. Bake 20 minutes, until golden
brown.
Lower temperature to 70°C (160°F).
Dry cookies for one hour with the oven
door slightly ajar.
These keep well in an airtight tin.

Helga Börjesson, Partille

Oatmeal-raisin cookies

PREPARATION TIME: *About 30 minutes*
OVEN TEMPERATURE: *175°C (350°F)*

YIELD: ABOUT 40 COOKIES
150 g (5 oz) unsalted
butter, softened
1 1/2 dl (2/3 cup) sugar
3 dl (1 1/4 cups)
rolled oats
1 teaspoon baking soda
1 1/2 dl (2/3 cup) raisins
1 1/2 dl (2/3 cup) flour

Beat butter and sugar until
light and fluffy. Add remaining ingredients,
mixing well. Form small balls and place 10
cm (4") apart on a greased cookie sheet. Press
down with a fork. Bake about 10 minutes.

Margit Brunnegård, Vårgårda

Sofi's crispy dreams

PREPARATION TIME: *About 45 minutes*
OVEN TEMPERATURE: *175°C (350°F)*

YIELD: ABOUT 50 COOKIES
100 g (3 1/2 oz) unsalted butter, softened
2 dl (3/4 cup) sugar
1 dl (1/3 cup) rapeseed oil
1 tablespoon vanilla sugar
(or 1 1/2 teaspoons extract)
1 teaspoon horn salt
(ammonium carbonate)
4 dl (1 2/3 cups) flour
2 tablespoons potato starch
2 dl (3/4 cup) cornflakes

Beat butter and sugar until light and fluffy.
Add oil, then add remaining ingredients,
mixing well. Form into 2 1/2 cm (1") balls
and place on a greased cookie sheet. Bake
on the middle oven shelf 13-15 minutes.
Cool, uncovered, on a rack.

Sofi Algervik, Alingsås

Brownies

PREPARATION TIME: *About 20 minutes*
OVEN TEMPERATURE: *175°C (350°F)*

YIELD: 15-20 SQUARES
50 g (1/3 cup) hazelnuts
2 eggs
1 1/2 dl (2/3 cup) sugar
100 g (3 1/2 oz) semi-sweet
chocolate
100 g (3 1/2 oz) unsalted butter, softened
1 1/2 dl (2/3 cup) flour
1/2 teaspoon baking powder

Grease and flour a 25x35 cm (10x14") pan
or line with baking parchment. Coarsely
chop nuts. Beat eggs and sugar until light
and lemon-colored. Chop chocolate and
melt in a double boiler or microwave oven.
Beat butter into egg mixture, then melted
chocolate. Fold in nuts, flour and baking
powder. Pour into prepared pan. Bake on
lowest oven shelf 7-10 minutes. Cool before
cutting into squares.

Monika Brunnegård, Asklanda

Gingerbread with ancho chile and almonds

PREPARATION TIME: *About one hour*
OVEN TEMPERATURE: *175°C (350°F)*

YIELD: ABOUT 60 COOKIES
2 1/4 dl (1 cup) sugar
1 dl (scant 1/2 cup) dark brown sugar
225 g (8 oz) unsalted butter, softened
1 egg
1/2 dl (3 1/2 tablespoons) golden syrup
2-3 teaspoons ground ancho chile pepper
2 teaspoons ground ginger
1 teaspoon ground cinnamon
1/2 teaspoon ground allspice
2 teaspoons baking soda
1/2 teaspoon salt
2 dl (3/4 cup) flaked almonds
about 5 dl (2 1/8 cups) flour

Combine both sugars and butter in a mixer with a dough hook. With the motor running, add egg, then syrup.
Add remaining ingredients, mixing well. Cover and refrigerate at least 30 minutes. Form into 3 cm (1 1/2") balls and place relatively far apart on a cookie sheet lined with baking parchment. Press down lightly. Bake about 10 minutes. Cool slightly before moving to a rack.

Jonas Borssén, Stockholm

Coconut macaroons

PREPARATION TIME: *About 30 minutes*
OVEN TEMPERATURE: *175°C (350°F)*

YIELD: ABOUT 30 COOKIES
50 g (3 tablespoons) unsalted butter
2 eggs
1 dl (scant 1/2 cup) sugar
200 g (7 oz) flaked coconut
100 g (3 1/2 oz) semi-sweet chocolate (optional)

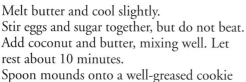

Melt butter and cool slightly.
Stir eggs and sugar together, but do not beat. Add coconut and butter, mixing well. Let rest about 10 minutes.
Spoon mounds onto a well-greased cookie sheet.
Bake about 10 minutes.
Remove cookies while still warm.
If desired, they can be dipped into melted chocolate.

Traditional recipe

Chocolate roll

PREPARATION TIME: *About 30 minutes*
OVEN TEMPERATURE: *250°C (475°C)*

YIELD: ABOUT 20 SLICES
3 eggs
1 1/2 dl (2/3 cup) sugar
5 tablespoons potato starch
1 tablespoon flour
2 tablespoons cocoa
1 teaspoon baking powder

Buttercream:
200 g (7 oz) unsalted butter, softened
1 1/2 dl (2/3 cup) confectioner's sugar
2 teaspoons vanilla sugar (or 1 teaspoon vanilla extract)
2 egg yolks

Sugar

Line a cookie sheet with baking parchment. Beat eggs and sugar until light and fluffy. Combine remaining ingredients and sift into egg mixture, mixing well. Spread mixture over the baking parchment. Bake about 10 minutes.
Sprinkle cake with sugar and cool slightly. Turn over and remove paper. Roll up loosely. Make buttercream: Beat butter, sugars and egg yolks to make a thick cream. Spread buttercream and roll up the cake lengthwise.

Traditional recipe

Traditional bread rings

EIGHT RINGS
50 g (3 tablespoons) butter
1 liter (4 cups) milk
50 g (1 3/4 oz) fresh yeast
1/2 tablespoon salt
2 tablespoons dark corn syrup
2 liters (8 cups) sifted rye flour
2 dl (1 cup) flour

During the first half of the 20th century, this was the most popular type of bread baked in Västergötland and Dalsland. It was especially good in a packed lunch.

PREPARATION TIME: *About 2 hours*   OVEN TEMPERATURE: *225°C (425°F)*

Melt butter in a saucepan. Add milk and heat to 37°C (98°F). Crumble yeast in a large mixing bowl and stir with a little milk. Add remaining liquid, salt, syrup and both kinds of flour. Knead until elastic, about 5 minutes in a mixer with a dough hook or 10 minutes by hand. Cover and let rise about 30 minutes. Punch down, knead, then divide into 8 pieces of equal size. Roll each into a round and prick with a skewer. Cut a hole in the center, cover and let rise 30 minutes more. Prick again and bake on center oven shelf 10 minutes. Cool covered.

Gunvor Fröberg, Anten

Seeded whole grain bread

FOUR BREADS
1 tablespoon caraway seed
1 tablespoon fennel seed
50 g (1 3/4 oz) fresh yeast
1 liter (4 cups) water
1 tablespoon salt
1/2 dl (3 1/2 tablespoons) vegetable oil
1/2 dl (3 1/2 tablespoons) dark corn syrup
1 1/2 dl (2/3 cup) unprocessed bran
1 1/2 dl (2/3 cup) sunflower seeds
1 dl (1/2 cup) coarse rye flour
2 liters (8 cups) flour

This is a classic recipe brought up-to-date with the addition of bran and sunflower seeds.

PREPARATION TIME: *About 90 minutes*
OVEN TEMPERATURE: *175°C (350°F)*

Crush spices in a mortar.
Crumble yeast in a large mixing bowl. Heat water to 37°C (98°F) and pour over yeast. Add salt, caraway seed, fennel, oil, syrup, bran, sunflower seeds, plus all the rye flour and most of the regular flour. Save a little for kneading.
Knead 5 minutes in a mixer with a dough hook or 10 minutes by hand. Turn out dough and divide into four pieces of equal size. Knead on a floured board. Form each into a round loaf. Cut a star in the center with a sharp knife. Cover and let rise 45 minutes. Bake on lowest oven shelf 35-40 minutes.

Janne Hedman, Lundsbrunn

Dalsland loaves

TWO LOAVES
1 1/2 liters (6 cups) sifted rye flour
2 dl (1 cup) rolled oats
4 teaspoons baking soda
2 teaspoons salt
9 dl (3 3/4 cups) 3% fat buttermilk or cultured milk
2 dl (3/4 cup) dark corn syrup
1 dl (1/2 cup) lingonberries or lingonberry compote

This recipe for a quick bread made without yeast comes from the county agricultural society's farm in Dalsland. The oats make the bread moist and add an additional local touch.

PREPARATION TIME: *About 70 minutes*
OVEN TEMPERATURE: *175°C (350°F)*

Grease and flour two loaf pans.
Combine dry ingredients in a mixing bowl. Add remaining ingredients, mixing well. Pour into prepared pans, spreading the batter evenly with a rubber spatula. Bake on lowest oven shelf about 60 minutes. Cover with aluminum foil toward the end of the cooking time. Brush the newly-baked loaves with lukewarm water. Cool covered.

Annika Dalbert, Åsnebyn

Sweet rye bread

FOUR LOAVES
1 dl (1/2 cup) plus 1 liter (4 cups) water
50 g (1 3/4 oz) fresh yeast
1 dl (scant 1/2 cup) vegetable oil
1 tablespoon salt
1 1/2 dl (2/3 cup) half light,
half dark corn syrup
1 tablespoon concentrated vinegar
23 dl (9 2/3 cups) sifted rye flour
1 liter (4 cups) flour
oil

This hearty rye bread comes from the southern part of the county. It is somewhat similar to classic Swedish sweet rye bread.

PREPARATION TIME: *About 2 hours*
OVEN TEMPERATURE: *200°C (400°F)*

Heat water to 37°C (98°F). Crumble yeast in 1 dl (1/2 cup) of the lukewarm water in a large mixing bowl. Add remaining water, oil, salt, syrup, and vinegar. Add almost all the flour and knead 5 minutes in a mixer with a dough hook or 10 minutes by hand. Cover and let rise 30 minutes.
Divide into four pieces of equal size and form into loaves. Line an oven tray with baking parchment. Brush each loaf with a little oil (so they won't stick together), then place in the tray. Cover and let rise 30 minutes.
Bake on lowest oven shelf 45 minutes. Cover with foil if they get too dark. Cool covered.

Elvy Karlsson, Björketorp

Farmer's loaves

FOUR LOAVES
100 g (3 1/2 oz) fresh yeast
6 dl (2 1/2 cups) 2% fat milk
1 dl (1/2 cup) honey
4 dl (1 2/3 cups) lingonberries
(or same amount lightly
sweetened compote,
but decrease the amount of
honey slightly)
1 teaspoon salt
13 dl (5 1/3 cups)
sifted rye flour
13 dl (5 1/3 cups)
four-grain flour

This bread is best when made with fresh lingonberries. They give the loaves a wonderful flavor and color. When the bread is so good, it can be eaten all on its own.

PREPARATION TIME: *About 3 hours*
OVEN TEMPERATURE: *175°C (350°F)*

Crumble yeast in a large mixing bowl. Heat milk and honey to 37°C (98°F) and pour over yeast. Stir in lingonberries. Add salt and most of the flour. Knead 5 minutes in a mixer with a dough hook or 10 minutes by hand. Cover and let rise 30 minutes.
Turn out onto a floured board, knead well and divide into four pieces of equal size. Form into loaves and place in a large greased oven tray. Cover and let rise 30 minutes. Bake on lowest oven shelf about 50 minutes. Cool covered.

Ingrid Månsson, Hajom

Oatmeal tea cakes

14 ROLLS
50 g (3 tablespoons) butter
5 dl (2 cups) milk
2 dl (3/4 cup) rolled oats
50 g (1 3/4 oz) fresh yeast
2 tablespoons corn syrup
1 egg
1/2 teaspoon salt
about 1 liter (4 cups) flour

A good way to guarantee moist bread is to use porridge as its base. This recipe uses freshly made oatmeal porridge, but years ago, leftover porridge did the job.

PREPARATION TIME: *70 minutes*   OVEN TEMPERATURE: *225°C (425°F)*

Melt butter in a saucepan. Add 2 1/2 dl (1 cup) of the milk and oatmeal. Cook to a thick porridge. Transfer to a large mixing bowl. Add remaining milk (cold), yeast, syrup, egg and salt.
Add almost all flour and knead 5 minutes in a mixer with a dough hook or 10 minutes by hand. Roll out on a floured board to a thickness of about 1 cm (1/2"). Cut out with a 10 cm (4") round cutter. Prick with a skewer. Cover and let rise 30 minutes.
Bake on center oven shelf 6-10 minutes. Cool covered.

Old recipe from Borås Museum

Spiced tea cakes

10 CAKES
50 g (1 3/4 oz) fresh yeast
100 g (3 1/2 oz) butter
1 liter (4 cups) milk
1 tablespoon anise seed
1 tablespoon fennel seed
1 dl (1/3 cup) light
corn syrup
1 tablespoon salt
2 tablespoons ground
dried bitter orange rind
5 dl (2 cups)
sifted rye flour
about 2 liters (8 1/3 cups)
flour

During the last century, thin flat breads were the norm along the coast. They could be eaten both fresh and dried, and fishermen took them along on voyages.

PREPARATION TIME: *About 2 hours*
OVEN TEMPERATURE: *275°C (525°F)*

Crumble yeast in a large mixing bowl. Melt butter, add milk and heat to 37°C (98°F). Pour over yeast and stir to dissolve. Crush anise and fennel seeds.
Stir in syrup, salt, spices, and rye flour. Add half the flour and combine. Add remaining flour and knead 5 minutes in a mixer with a dough hook or 10 minutes by hand. Cover and let rise 30 minutes. Punch down, cover and let rise 30 more minutes. Turn out onto a floured board and knead a few minutes. Divide into 10 pieces of equal size and roll into balls. Cover and let rise 20 minutes.
Grease cookie sheets. Roll out each piece of dough into a round large enough to fit two on a cookie sheet. Repeat. Prick with a skewer. Bake on top oven shelf about 5-7 minutes.
Stack and cool covered.

Traditional recipe

Cold-rise carrot bread with honey

24 SQUARES
50 g (1 3/4 oz) fresh yeast
1/2 dl (3 1/2 tablespoons)
runny honey
3/4 dl (1/3 cup) liquid
margarine
1 dl (1/2 cup) creamed
cottage cheese
3 dl (1 1/4 cups)
shredded carrots
5 dl (2 cups) milk
1/2 teaspoon salt
1 1/2 liters (6 1/4 cups)
unbleached bread flour

These lovely breakfast rolls owes their beautiful color and flavor to carrots. They are easy to make, but they do have to rise overnight. The first one up in the morning gets to bake them and brew coffee or tea. Do not use dry yeast in this recipe.

PREPARATION TIME: *50 minutes plus rising overnight*
OVEN TEMPERATURE: *200°F (400°C)*

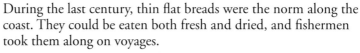

OLD ADAGE
"Thin slices of bread steal butter"

Crumble yeast in a large mixing bowl.
Add honey, margarine, cheese, carrots, milk and salt. Combine well. Add almost all the flour. Knead 5 minutes in a mixer with a dough hook or 10 minutes by hand.
Spread dough with floured hands in a large oven pan lined with baking parchment. Cut into 24 squares.
Cover with plastic wrap and refrigerate overnight.
The next day, remove the pan from the refrigerator and preheat the oven. Let rise at room temperature while the oven is heating up. Cut squares over again, if necessary.
Bake on lowest oven shelf 20 minutes.
Cool covered on a rack.

Sofia Hidendahl, Östra Frölunda

From bark bread to bake-off

BREAD HAS ALWAYS BEEN A mainstay of man's diet. It has been eaten fresh or dried, – "reused" in soups, or as French toast, poultry stuffing, ground meat extenders and much more.
Food baked in bread or served with bread has always been popular – whether called ciabatta, bagels, baguette, focaccia, injera, pita, or hot-dog buns. Intermediate varieties include taco shells, pancakes, pirogies, lasagna noodles, wraps, tortillas, pizza crust, and thin sheets of unleavened bread. Nearly all contain wheat flour, oil, yeast, salt and water.

These ingredients (with the exception of yeast) have been used in bread for thousands of years. Remains of bread have been found in Babylonian and Egyptian tombs. The tomb of Ramses III, dating back to about 1100 B.C., features a wall painting of a large bakery. Just before the birth of Christ, there were approximately 300 bakeries in Rome.

The oldest known Swedish bread, dating back to the third century, was found in excavations at Helgö in Lake Mälaren. The first known picture of bread in Europe can be seen on the Bayeux Tapestry, dating from the twelfth century.

The Vikings learned about different kinds of ovens in their travels, and they brought this knowledge back to Scandinavia. Until that time, flatbread was baked on flat stones or iron griddles.

The Vikings also used bread as a plate. Their bread was hard and compact and was softened by the food served on it, which is still popular in Scandinavia today.

Nordic peoples first learned about yeast during the Middle Ages, but civilizations to the south had known about it for thousands of years. As Scandinavians began to brew beer, they also began to use brewer's yeast in baking. Nordic bread was more like fried porridge than bread. Even now, such

Bread has always been a cheap and nutritious food. In 1732, Linnaeus wrote a pamphlet with 20 kinds of emergency-bread for the poor – and Alströmer preached that boiled potatoes should be used to extend bread. He had gotten his recipe from Ireland.

Bark bread was considered to be fortifying, and people had known for a long time that it made them feel good. Modern Japanese research also indicates that bark bread has health benefits. But today, it costs SEK 15,000 for a kilo of bark extract. It takes one tall pine to produce one kilo of extract.

primitive bread – rieska – is baked in Norrland. The line between porridge and bread is quite vague. Porridge, beer and bread all contain the same basic ingredients.

Bread has a sacred aspect in many religions. When we say "our daily bread", we really mean all food. In the same vein, it makes sense that the islanders of Raroia in Oceania prayed: "Give us this day our daily fish".

There have always been many different kinds of breads. These varied according with respect to where people lived and to which

social class they belonged. In a diary entry from December 20, 1828, Märta Helena Reenstierna wrote about Christmas baking at Årsta farm. Rye bread, two kinds of wort and two of wheat bread were made, as well as 70 cakes – flattened, rather thick disks with holes in the center for hanging on a rod up in the rafters. All fine baking, cookies and such, was done in the afternoon. In 1835, she wrote that after bread had been given to employees and relatives in Stockholm, there were still 1560 "cakes" left.

In contrast to this abundance, the following notice appeared in a report from the municipality of Mellby, Västra Götaland, on March 25, 1869. As a preventive measure, one bread would be distributed to each poor person in the area. Half rye and half oats was considered a good mixture. There was no mention of how often this would take place.

Heating the ovens was heavy work, and

partly for that reason, baking was done infrequently. During the 1920s, in Kinnarumma, Västra Götaland, a man recorded his family's baking routine. They often made a batch of around 300 "cakes". At Christmas, they made even more, hoping the bread would last until Easter. They used mostly mixed grain and oat flour and made fairly thick disks with holes in the center. Wheat bread and thin unleavened bread or crackers were reserved for the upper-classes and the clergy and seldom made by average people except for Christmas. Many people still consider white bread a luxury and regard whole grain bread as everyday food.

In her famous cookbook, Kajsa Warg confirms that winter was too cold for baking, and in summer, there were other important things to do. In spring and fall, there was enough water to run the mills, and for that reason, these were suitable times for baking in large quantities.

There has always been a wide range of breads in Sweden, partly because our country has several climate zones, and because of cultural contacts. Barley grows well in the north but it does not have any rising ability, thus the popularity of flat breads

Rye has been the most common grain in the east and south, while oats were grown in Skaraborg. Wheat was cultivated on a small scale, only by well-off people in the plains. Everywhere, though, cereals were essential to the storehouse economy. Coarse flour, made of mixed grains or oats, was used in traditional hole-breads during the week, while sifted flour was baked into breads with a finer texture for weekends and holidays. Loaf breads were for festive occasions.

TRADITIONAL HOLE BREAD

The same kinds of bread were baked in southern Älvsborg and Dalsland as in Skaraborg: hole-breads all week and thicker loaves on weekends and special occasions.

In Bohuslän, dry thin crackers were the

norm. They stored well on fishing boats. Similar breads are still being produced today. Of course, we buy them soft and eat them while fresh. Years ago, they were dried and could remain edible for months or even years.

Drying bread was a widespread method of preservation. It insured against crop failures and accidents that could affect the food supply. The best thin crackers are baked in a stone oven and have a slightly burnt flavor. One sort, Hönö tea cakes, even tastes of cardamom.

A kind of bread similar to a dark rye is found in Bohuslän. The coarse, crusty loaves are called "sour bangers". Split and dried, they were ideal for long journeys at sea.

HÖNÖ COMMUNITY CENTER

HÖNÖ TEA CAKES

Bread was sometimes flavored with honey or brewer's wort, which was sweet – and later syrup or sugar. But the sweetness also could come from badly preserved flour that had begun to sprout (or malt). After World War II, Swedes were advised to add 500 grams of syrup for every liter of liquid in bread dough, as a source of energy. That may be partly why Swedes prefer sweet bread. This bread was often flavored with fennel and caraway and sometimes imported spices, budget permitting.

The custom of giving neighbors a "bread-sample" was fairly widespread. Different households baked at different times, so this was a good way to enjoy fresh bread more often.

Storing bread was a problem before freezers became common household appliances. Hole-breads were threaded onto poles under the roof, safe from hungry children, mice and other household "pets". There, too, it was warm and dry. Bread baked as loaves and other kinds of soft bread were stored in chests in attics where

grain was kept, or in bread boxes and bins. They dried out quickly and had to be softened in soup or in cultured milk.

Older cookbooks include few recipes for everyday bread, since authors felt that standard bread recipes were common knowledge and needed no explanation. Those old recipes that do exist are variations on wort bread, and of bread containing saffron or other spices. Almost all of them are made from sour dough.

Over less than 50 years, respect for bread has increased enormously. We remember our grandmothers in white aprons, with kerchiefs round their heads, baking for many days in a row. The men made sure that the right kind of wood was available, and they maintained an even heat in the large oven or wood stove.

Compare that with today, when we can run into any gas station or convenience store, every hour of every day, and buy fresh bread

We may enjoy the wonderful aroma – but not the satisfaction of having baked the bread ourselves.

Gunvor Fröberg

"And now maybe a little schnapps?"

WHEN SOCRATES AND Plato drank, they diluted their wine with water, and plenty of it. This did not prevent them from getting tipsy. The sun was hot in their homeland, and they needed to consume a lot of liquid.

According to my Latin teacher, the Romans drank wine unmixed during the winter, but his substitute said this was not really the case. For a true Roman – the substitute wanted to be seen as such – it was vulgar to drink wine undiluted. No empires were built by winos.

But this was just what our forefathers did, for the old Swedes were famous drinkers. Their empire was short-lived, yet it fell apart because there were so few Swedes and they had limited resources, not because they drank so much.

Our reputation for intemperance, however, was already established by then. Even Shakespeare knew. He wrote of the noisy toast the Swedish king makes to Prince Hamlet, saying in effect:

"Bring me the tankard! Let the kettle-drum announce to the trumpet, the trumpet to our cannoneer out there, the cannons to the sky and the sky to the earth: now the king drinks to Hamlet's health."

Hamlet's friend, Horatio, wonders what could possibly be going on. Hamlet explains that the king is having a good binge, giddy with vanity. For every gulp he takes of Rhine wine, drums and trumpets declare that he is not in the habit of being a disappointing carouser.

Still, adds Hamlet, although I am a child of the country, violating this custom seems to me more honorable than keeping it. Such a wild life shames us among other peoples to the east and west. They call us drunkards and swine.

In the east, yes. A old book of mine states that the Swedes learned the art of making liquor – that is, of distilling – from the Russians. But the king drinks wine from the Rhineland. Neither Greeks, Romans, nor medieval northern Europeans could make spirits, not even on stage. Naturally, Hamlet

AT THE STATE STORE
*"Say, goo'day to you, Igust,
that was a while ago I last saw
you – but hoppin' herrin', how
your hair's gone gray!"*

*"Yep, out of plain fright –
it was when I heard the news
that they'd raised the price
of schnapps to 1:45 a liter."*

Olaus Magnus was a scholar, not just a bookworm. He had journeyed in Sweden and Norway, even selling letters of indulgence. He knew the popular customs of his countrymen well, and if the situation demanded it, he defended his country's honor as a true patriot.

I have no doubt whatsoever about his statement that Norsemen, when feasting, could place huge tankards of beer or wine on their heads and dance in a ring. In this manner, they showed their capacity not only to consume in quantity, but also their ability to tolerate what they drank – that is, they kept their balance.

A Swede, who is used to our present-day legal limit, will probably find it harder to believe Olaus when he says that, during a feast, good men were obliged to honor the king by rising and seeing who could first empty, in one or more draughts, a Capitoline tankard of beer. A glass of beer is forty percent of a liter (less than two cups), but a Capitoline tankard held 26 liters!

Our folklore is full of drinking tales. The strange thing about them is that they are funny. But, drunkenness is not a bit funny. At best, it is funny to see people loosening up and having fun.

One of my favorite anecdotes is from writer Albert Engström. A train has just arrived at a station. Down climbs a man on crutches, all bandaged up.

A bystander asks: "Wedding or funeral?"

The visitor replies: "Baptism!"

When relatives and friends gather for a festive event, they drink. When they drink, they get happy, and in extreme cases, furious.

is referring to Danish drinking, but nothing indicates that Swedes were, or should have been, judged any less harshly.

Shakespeare may have heard of Olaus Magnus' "History of the Nordic Peoples". In it, the exiled author wrote about our drinking customs.

Olaus Magnus had been the dean of Strängnäs cathedral, but left the country when Gustav Vasa confiscated church property and attacked the faith.

The pope appointed him archbishop in exile, an extraordinary office. He wrote his great book in Rome, in Latin, of course, so the entire educated world could read about us – and it was soon translated into colloquial languages.

This is moderately funny. The real humor is in the unexpected answer.

But nobody needs anecdotes in order to show respect for schnapps. As a schoolboy, I rented a room with a family. One day I opened the door to a man who was looking for the father of the house. He wanted to return a half-bottle which he owed. The gentlemen talked for quite a while. When the stranger left, he took the bottle with him.

The housekeeper told me later that the man was very trustworthy and reliable. If he promised to repay on a certain day, he would do so. On the other hand, he always borrowed again immediately.

Beer, wine and liquor stimulate aggressiveness. Our cities would be much more peaceful without alcohol. On the other hand, they have never been so peaceful as in our time. This is worth remembering whenever we read about our violent society.

Before the era of hamburgers and pasta, a Swedish meal began in front of the liquor table or cabinet. There, people stood and ate – or rather, the men ate. The culinary travelogues I have read were all written by men.

Schnapps was always served before the actual meal, and tidbits, such as smoked eel, cheese, herring, anchovies, smoked ham, and caviar, were placed alongside. A really elegant spread featured flavored liquor and glasses of different size – up to eight per guest. Everyone started with the largest glass and worked down to the smallest, the little pearl. After that, dinner was served

The toasts began just before dessert, writes the traveler. One had to respond, even when toasted by every single person around the

table. For the present-day reader, this sounds as if the nation was drinking itself to death.

Even Lucia Day had its special drinks. Lucia and her procession of maidens appear to be visions of temperance, surrounded as they are by the smell of coffee and sweet rolls. But N. P. Ödman from Värmland, who wrote his memoirs in the early 1900s, knew more about the procession's rustic character.

Lucia was a western Swedish custom. At Uppsala university, only those from Värmland and Gothenburg celebrated it. The other student clubs long made conceited efforts to join in.

The club elected the prettiest newcomers of the season to be Lucia. N. P. Ödman particularly remembers Anton Nyström from Gothenburg, an utter beauty with whom numerous students fell in love.

Worth remembering, too, were "the nowadays so well-known wholesaler and friend of royalty, Carl Wijk" and the young future officer, Wikland, fresh and pink-cheeked as a rose in bloom.

The Lucia procession visited the officers and honorary members of the club in their homes, and Lucia poured them glasses of cognac to ward off the evening chill. Then they proceeded onward, with musical accompaniment, to the club hall and break-fast: spareribs, ham, pork sausage, shandy and mulled wine. The professors tried to outdo each other with compliments to Lucia, in her crown of candles, who accepted them, blushing and smiling.

To clarify matters, I must point out that the first female student was enrolled at the university in 1872. Before that, it was necessary to recruit one of the beautiful young men at hand.

Understandably, the party got out of hand. Lucia became as shrill as her followers and her feminine charm vanished. After all, she was forced to respond to all the toasts.

How customs have mellowed! From Gothenburg and Värmland, Lucia has spread across the country. Now she can even be introduced Nobel Prize laureates and their families.

It has been a long time since any host had to discuss before dinner, whether he and his guests should drink like men or like beasts.

"Like men!" said the guests in unison, insulted by the host's crudity. "Good," said the host, "animals never drink more than they need."

I do not feel that foreigners have any reason to be upset about our drinking any longer. As long as we stay at home, our habits are moderate. Things get worse when Swedes, particularly young ones, travel abroad.

We have an extremely peculiar and absurd relationship with alcohol, both laughing about it and lamenting it. We feel its destructive power, but also know that it spreads joy. This ambivalent attitude makes us both reject it and accept it at the same time.

In Dublin, I once heard a lecture about the Irish economy, part of which was about the increase in exports of Irish whiskey. Afterward, I wondered why I was so bewildered, until I realized why. This was the first time in my life – at age fifty – that I had heard someone, without hesitation and apologies, express pleasure at an increase in alcohol consumption.

One of my sources insists that schnapps was known in Sweden already during the early sixteenth century. So that's how long we have fought with restrictions, taxation, health care, imprisonment, and the other aspects of alcohol consumption. Gustav Vasa is said to have forbidden the distillation of spirits after the failed harvest of 1550. But, he had to give way to public opinion, which

he was not used to doing. People complained and the army was a strong pressure group.

The history of Swedish schnapps is an endless swing between bans and permits. Schnapps is a coveted article of consumption, but few people consider it indispensable, and even more regard it as harmful. Thus, it is a fine target for taxation. A fee for manufacturing it was first introduced in 1638.

In his book, "The History of the Royal Academy of Science", Sten Lindroth writes that no subject could compete with schnapps in popularity. The scarcity of grain was a threat. Other raw materials were sought – potatoes, obviously – and even rowanberries and other berries were suggested.

The crop failure of 1771 brought a ban on all manufacture and sales of spirits. In 1775, royal distilleries were started instead: in other words, state alcohol factories. Alcohol was allowed to be sold, but people began to distill their own, and the law was abolished. So it has been and so it shall continue. And soon we'll be allowed to shop on Saturdays again.

But we don't blame failed harvests any more.

Sune Örnberg

The county's best schnapps

WHAT WOULD MIDSUMMER be without a glass of schnapps? Or Christmas dinner's array of delicacies, which almost demands something strong at intervals to get us through it all? Out of the question, we think, even though we must handle strong drinks with the caution they demand. An awareness of the tragic moments in the history of Swedish schnapps should not hinder us from enjoying the combination of food and schnapps today. Beer and schnapps belong on the western Swedish table. As the next pages show, there is great interest in the drink itself and in "creating" one's own schnapps. We recommend making one or two kinds of schnapps, for example, in good time before Christmas, and then preparing a small festive dinner to test them. Everything depends on when you can obtain the sometimes rather exotic ingredients that must be added. Just remember that, once you have strained off the flavorings, the schnapps becomes ever better the longer it matures. About 15 years ago, I had the pleasure of meeting Albert Sandklef, who wrote the

Herring in the ocean with cod and other fishes takes a nice cold drink whenever the hell it wishes

MELODY: THE MAIDEN IN THE RING...

classic "Thirty Sorts of Spiced Schnapps". We were expanding the book, and I had asked for three new recipes. In his kitchen on Föreningsgatan in Gothenburg, we sat and philosophized about life in general and schnapps in particular. We tried one of his favorite sorts, a mild bitter, seasoned with shore wormwood. Almost dark-brown and a bit thick in consistency, it was velvet on the throat and created the same feeling as hot chocolate on a cold winter day. The wormwood flavor took a while to arise, but once it did, its strength was intense, without being too bitter. My relationship to Bitter Drops has changed considerably since then. The conversation at the kitchen table ended with Albert Sandklef musing: "Abstinence may be a virtue, but I don't store my schnapps longer than ten years!"

Recipes were sent from all over the county for this book's competition. The following schnapps recipes are the best in Västra Götaland, according to our jury. Don't be afraid to try slightly different mixtures of spices. They can lead to exciting experiences. And, for the sake of flavor, it is more important to recall what Albert Sandklef said about storing his own schnapps!

Gunnar Stenmar

Golden glitter

Summer's last gasp

Golden glitter

INGREDIENTS:
15 dried juniper berries
10 cm (4") juniper twig
7 dl (3 cups) pure grain alcohol

PREPARATION:
Crush berries and place in a bottle along with the juniper twig.
Add alcohol and let steep one week.
Strain and serve with a fresh juniper twig with ripe berries in the carafe or glass.

Rosa Almvide and
Ingalill Åmark-Söderblom, Lerum

Summer's last gasp

THE COOKBOOK
CONTEST
SECOND PRIZE
SCHNAPPS

INGREDIENTS:
70 dl (3 cups) pure grain alcohol
1 teaspoon caraway seed
25 anise seeds
5 fresh peppermint leaves
5 dried juniper berries, halved

PREPARATION:
Combine 1 dl (1/2 cup) alcohol with remaining ingredients in a glass jar with a lid. Shake at least twice a day. After two days, strain extract into a carafe and add remaining alcohol.
This drink tastes even better after it has matured for a month.
It tastes best slightly chilled.

Bo Karlsson, Karlskoga,
a summer resident of Lysekil

Rosehip schnapps

Wild rowan schnapps

Rosehip schnapps

INGREDIENTS:
*3 dl (1 1/4 cups) dried,
cleaned rosehips
7 dl (3 cups) pure grain alcohol
2 tablespoons fresh lemon juice
2 teaspoons confectioner's sugar*

PREPARATION:
Bring rosehips and water to just
cover to a boil. Cook until it
turns to mush. Transfer to a jar
with a lid and add 6 dl (2 1/2
cups) alcohol.
Store in a cold, dark place for
4-5 months.
Add 1 dl (1/2 cup) alcohol.
Strain, then pour through a
coffee filter.
Flavor with lemon juice and
confectioner's sugar.
Pour into bottle, seal and store
in a cold, dark place for at least
two more months.

Anneli Gustavsson, Stockholm

Wild rowan schnapps

INGREDIENTS:
*5 dl (2 cups) water
2 dl (3/4 cup) frost-nipped
rowanberries
7 dl (3 cups) pure grain alcohol
3 cm (1 1/4") vanilla bean, split
3 star anise*

PREPARATION:
Bring water to a boil, then add
berries. Drain immediately and
let berries dry for a while.
Add alcohol, berries, vanilla
bean and star anise in a bottle or
jar with a lid.
Let steep up to two weeks.
Strain and pour into a bottle.
This snapps tastes even better
after it has been stored for a
few months.

Maria Christensson, Brastad

Alingsås aquavit

*Red currant
holiday schnapps*

Alingsås aquavit

INGREDIENTS:
*10-15 heather sprigs
7 dl (3 cups) pure
grain alcohol*

PREPARATION:
Pick heather just
before it blooms.
Combine 1/3 of the
heather with 2/3 of
the alcohol. Let steep
3-4 weeks. Strain and add 5-10
parts alcohol.
Store 3-6 months.
Heather is Västergötland's regional
flower. Heather schnapps is
considered therapeutic and is
recommended for stomach
ailments.

*Ulf Larsson and AM Alströmer,
Alingsås*

THE COOKBOOK
CONTEST
FIRST PRIZE
SCHNAPPS

Red currant
holiday schnapps

INGREDIENTS:
*About 5 dl (2 cups) red currants
7 dl (3 cups) pure grain alcohol*

PREPARATION:
Place cleaned, ripe berries in a
bottle. Add alcohol to cover.
One bottle of alcohol should be
enough for two bottles of
berries. Let steep three months.
Strain off berries and store for
three years. After that time, it
becomes reddish-brown with
heavy sediment. Strain through
a coffee filter. For every six parts
essence, add four parts alcohol.
The fresh flavor of this drink is
perfect with traditional Swedish
Christmas food.

Lars Skoglund, Lidingö

Västgöta schnapps I

Västgöta schnapps 1

INGREDIENTS:
7 dl (3 cups)
pure grain alcohol
20 ripe wild cherries
6 wild cherry leaves
1 dl (1/2 cup)
white currants
6 currant leaves
6 sugar cubes

THE COOKBOOK
CONTEST
THIRD PRIZE
SCHNAPPS

PREPARATION:
Combine all ingredients in a
bottle and let steep one month.
Strain. Let steep one more
month. Strain, It is ready to
drink, but it is even better after it
has been stored 3-6 months.

Lennart Granqvist, Tidaholm

Scurvy cure

INGREDIENTS:
70-100 g (2 1/2-3 1/2 oz)
scurvy weed
7 dl (3 cups) pure grain alcohol

PREPARATION:
Puree leaves in a food processor.
Add alcohol and let steep one
week. Strain.

Scurvy weed has such an
interesting flavor that I have
given up all attempts to combine
it – with spirits, it forms an ideal
marriage.
This plant grows on all beaches
facing the sea. It used to be eaten
by sailors to prevent scurvy.
But since it contains mustard oil,
it has a rather strong flavor.
Two or three rosettes are enough
for whole bottle of alcohol.
Do not use the roots.

Göran Michanek, Gothenburg

Golden heather schnapps

INGREDIENTS:
5 tablespoons (1/3 cup) heather
flowers stripped from the stalks
7 dl (3 cups) pure grain alcohol

PREPARATION:
Cover flowers with alcohol.
Let steep one week, then
strain off flowers.
Store in a dark place one
more week.
When serving, garnish with
more flowers.

Rosa Almvide and
Ingalill Åmark-Söderblom, Lerum

Swamp dew

INGREDIENTS:
3 dl (1 1/4 cups) frost-nipped
cranberries
7 dl (3 cups) pure grain alcohol

PREPARATION:
Combine berries and alcohol.
Store in a cold place for 10 days.
Strain and use immediately.
The drained berries can be
served with meat dishes.

Rosa Almvide and
Ingalill Åmark-Söderblom, Lerum

Fredriksdal schnapps

INGREDIENTS:
1 teaspoon dried coriander
1 teaspoon star anise
2 teaspoons dried peppermint leaves
7 dl (3 cups) pure grain alcohol

PREPARATION:
Place spices in a clean bottle.
Add twice the amount of alcohol
needed to cover spices.
Let steep three days, then pour
through a coffee filter.
Pour concentrate back into
original bottle.

Magnus Skoglundh, Gothenburg

Västgöta schnapps 2

Västgöta schnapps 2

INGREDIENTS:
7 dl (3 cups) pure grain alcohol
2 clusters tansy
20 blossoming heather sprigs
2 teaspoons honey

PREPARATION:
Combine and let steep three days.
Strain. Stir in honey and it's ready to drink.

Lennart Granqvist, Tidaholm

We have always been good at making cheese in Västra Götaland

SINCE THE BEGINNING OF civilization, bread, cheese and wine have been the mainstays of the diet in the area around the Mediterranean. There is no doubt that cheese has played an important role in our heritage, and it still does.

We probably ate cheese even before we learned to use milk as a beverage. That happened long before man's transition from hunter-gatherer to nomad-farmer. Weapons were so primitive that he often had to settle for smaller beasts, such as the calves of wild cattle. Our ancestors most likely consumed the stomach contents of the animals they killed. The stomach of a newly-killed calf frequently contained milk that had curdled and formed a kind of fresh cheese curds in contact with the rennet in its stomach.

Knowledge of cheese production is believed to have come from Asia, through Europe and up to Scandinavia, several thousand years before Christ. In our country, a chalet culture arose, in which

cheese was considered essential to the diet. Milk from cows, goats and sheep was used to make cheese.

Until the 18th century, a large percentage of the cheese produced in Sweden was made from sheep milk. Today, very little cheese is produced from sheep and goat milk.

These people from Västra Götaland

We have always been good at making cheese in Västra Götaland. Olaus Magnus wrote: *"Among all those who live in the North, the people of Västra Götaland are held in the highest esteem for their cheese. No one can compare with them...Here they make such large cheeses that two strong man can barely manage to carry one block at a time, even a short distance."*

In order to make a really big cheese, which took a lot of milk, neighbors collaborated. Olaus Magnus continued: *"During the summer, they gather at the home of whoever makes the cheese, and a large quantity of milk has been brought there for that*

purpose. The milk is boiled in huge cauldrons, rennet is added, and the curds are pressed into wooden molds, mostly square in shape."

Such activities took place all over Sweden and in many other landscapes as well. Cheese was manufactured for the area's pastor as part of his salary and as a tithe to the church.

During the late 1800's, a number of break-throughs contributed to the industrialization of cheese-making. Gustaf de Laval invented the separator in 1878, and pasturization of milk, which killed undesirable bacteria, became widespread. Commercial production of lactic acid cultures and rennet also began around this time.

Suggestions and ideas

It is a good idea to use aged cheeses in sauces and pasta dishes because it melts better and does not become stringy. Recommended cheeses include aged *Swedish prästost* and *Parmesan*. These are used primarily to add flavor to food, because texture is not so important.

A milder cheese is better in pizza and au gratin dishes, because a stringier and thicker consistency when melted is desirable. Swedish cheeses of this type include *mild prästost* and *gräddost*. Aged cheeses with more flavor can be used in au gratin dishes, but these kinds of cheese tend to spread out more when melted.

Many fresh cheeses are used in cooking and baking. They are excellent in pies, breads, and desserts, because they pair so well with sweet flavors, such as cloudberries and pineapple.

In Sweden, *soft white-rinded cheeses such as Brie and Camembert, and blue cheeses* are used primarily on cheese trays. Both kinds, however, are also very good in cooking. Camembert can be heated and served with cloudberries for desert, and blue cheeses can add flavor to pasta sauce.

Swedes eat hard cheese primarily on open-face sandwiches – and we eat about seven million cheese sandwiches every single day.

Tomas Bengtsson

Everyone loves
porcelain from Lidköping

IN 1898, HE GOTHENBURG Porcelain Factory was established and became Västra Götaland's first porcelain industry. The factory was at Hisingen, not far from where the stream at Kville joins the Göta River. It was a good location, because most raw materials came by boat.

Granted, true porcelain had already been manufactured in Sweden for more than 40 years, but the Gothenburg factory made technically less complicated stoneware. And it did that successfully.

Many transfer patterns were imported from abroad, but when one was copied in the local atelier, the pieces were marked "original". The first pattern traced in the atelier became one of the most popular, best known and loved china patterns in Sweden. It was called Anna, after the wife of the founder and first owner of the factory, Simeon Schwartz. In the beginning, the Anna pattern was produced in lilac, but in 1914, the factory adopted green and the pattern became known as Green Anna.

The Gothenburg Porcelain Factory remained independent until 1914, when it was acquired by Rörstrand AB, which had

been in Stockholm since 1726. The new owner, however, gave its subsidiary a great deal of freedom to develop new products in the style and materials that were the factory specialties.

The Lidköping Porcelain Factory was one of three which established between 1910 and 1920. Nyman's Porcelain Painters, at Kinneviken, had been active since the turn of the century. They specialized in the painting and firing of German porcelain blanks, and business prospered. Good sales figures and a favorable business climate inspired the owners to establish a new factory covering the entire manufacturing process – from clay to finished product.

In 1929, the factory made an 890-piece dinner services as an engagement present for Crown Prince Olav of Norway and Princess Märtha of Sweden from the women of Skaraborg county.

During the latter part of the 1920's, there were several events that were important for the porcelain factories in Gothenburg and Lidköping. For a number of reasons, Rörstrand decided to transfer base of operations to its subsidiary in Gothenburg. In 1926, the Stockholm factory closed, and

Rörstrand's entire production line disappeared. Products manufactured in Gothenburg, such as Green Anna, now acquired the Rörstrand mark.

Rörstrand's other classic from this period is the East India service. In 1931, Gothenburg planned to celebrate the 200th anniversary of the East India Company. Rörstrand wanted commemorate the event with a new pattern in the spirit of the original style. One day, Emmy Almström was looking for her husband, Knut, at the office. He was out, and while she waited, she found a few shards of Chinese porcelain in a display cabinet. She removed them and wrote on a note telling her husband that this would be the pattern for the new service. Knut Almström agreed, and development began immediately. Modelers and draftsmen were able to present the new model in record time. A competition was held to decide on the name, just after the pattern was introduced.

This was the beginning of a new, very successful chapter in Rörstrand's history. Fredrik Wethje was only 28 years old when he became Managing Director, but he had a solid education from Germany and practical training from the Arabia factory in Finland. Relatively unencumbered by older perspectives, he decided to apply the most modern methods to production.

In the fall of 1936, he opened a new factory, and since then, Rörstrand has been considered a Lidköping company. Production continued in Gothenburg for three more years. Among other things, it made paste for the production of stoneware in Lidköping. This was transported by rail in specially painted blue and yellow cars marked with Rörstrand's logo.

At first, there were only 120 workers at the new plant, but the number grew rapidly. Once Fredrik Wethje had a modern and functional factory, he could devote himself to his other great interest – developing the factory's art and design departments.

In 1976, Rörstrand celebrated its 250th anniversary. On June 16, the King opened a new museum in connection with the factory, as well as an extensive exhibition at Läckö Castle. Visitors came from far and wide. When the gates closed at the end of August, a total of 153,000 people had visited the exhibition. And that record still stands. Extensive coverage by the mass media helped boost the number of visitors.

Friday, October 25, 1991, was another important date in the history of Rörstrand. It marked the opening of a new factory for the production of feldspar porcelain in the old plant from 1936. This was the first step in a thorough transformation of the company, which was gradually implemented in the intervening years and has been one of Rörstrand's most extensive investments. And Rörstrand received even more publicity when it introduced the Nobel pattern, designed by Karin Björquist, at the Nobel Prize banquet on December 10 that same year.

Kristian Lundgren

The history of Västra Götaland

THE GOTHS, WHO LIVED IN THE region now called Västra Götaland, are first mentioned in written sources during the second century. They settled in Falbygden and along the southern shore of Vänern, and in Dalsland which is a continuation of the West Göta plain. These isolated settlements had little contact with the outside world. There was a route over Vänern, but otherwise, communications were few.

Västra Götaland has been historically important since our earliest history. There are many archaeological remains, including the richest hoards of pre-Roman gold in Sweden.

Among the attractions at Västra Götaland Museum in Skara are sixteen bronze shields found in the water at Vänervik. Some had been submerged for more than 3000 years.

Many Goths participated in Viking raids. A relic from that period is a cargo vessel which was found at Äskekärr in Starrkärs parish in 1933. It is now in the Gothenburg City Museum.

During the eleventh century, the realm was united and Christianity established. Goths and Swedes acquired a common king. At this time, Västra Götaland became the destination of missionaries from the west, and it was the first province to be Christianized.

For a long time, the Göta River separated Västra Götaland and Bohuslän in Norway. It was not until the 1200s that Sweden established a corridor to the North Sea at the river's mouth. During the 900s, Västra Götaland's first city, Lödöse, was established along the river and grew into a dominant trading center during the 1100's. About a mile to the south was its Norwegian counterpart, Kungahalla. On the Swedish side of the river, in Skepplanda parish, was Grönköping – not to be confused with today's fiction town of the same name.

The Norwegians, however, could block Lödöse's exit to the North Sea, and they did so, especially after Bohus fortress was erected in the early 1300s. The Swedes responded in two ways: They moved Lödöse, and they built a fortress at the mouth of the river.

This corridor area was always contested, and small skirmishes between Sweden and Denmark were not at all unusual. Danish armies regularly invaded Västra Götaland and eventually erected many defense walls and fortresses. These give some idea of the strategic significance of the landscape.

In those days, Västra Götaland was not only a battlefield, but also a place of peace. During the eleventh century, many state churches were built in bishopric of Skara. A number of them are still standing, as can be seen in Hedared outside Alingsås.

In 1621, the present city of Gothenburg was established at the mouth of the river in the Swedish corridor. At that time, Bohuslän and Halland both were under Danish rule. Gothenburg became a fortified city, one of the strongest in Europe. Shortly thereafter, it began to develop as a trading center with active connections to the west.

The 1600s were Sweden's period of greatness. Bohuslän and Halland were

A. *1100–1389.* B. *1389–1520.* C. *1500s*

D. *1600s* E. *1700s.* F. *1800s.*

annexed through the Treaty of Roskilde in 1658, and Gothenburg was no longer squeezed in a narrow corridor. Over the next 150 years, the Danes tried to reconquer lost territory, so Västra Götaland became a war zones many more times.

By 1700, Gothenburg had about 4,000 citizens. A century later, it was the second city of the realm, with 12,000 people. This was an economic boom time, and wooden buildings were constructed, softening its gray fortress image.

Gothenburg was coming under strong British influence. It was particularly intense at the Swedish East India Company, established in  1731. In a magazine article published in 1766, Gothenburg was referred to as "Little London":

"If our city is called Little Amsterdam because of its neat and tidy facilities, there is reason, in view of the hedges, gardens and oaks planted on city land, to foresee that Gothenburg may in future be called Little London."

British cooking had scarcely earned a reputation for culinary excellence, but British drinks were thus all the more outstanding. Tea, punsch and porter all became popular in Little London during this time.

The eighteenth century was a flourishing age for Gothenburg and Bohuslän, and many wealthy merchants and other citizens established charitable organization in their names. One of these, the Sahlgrenska Hospital, still exists today.

There were literally tons of herring off the shores of Bohuslän, and to exploit the enormous catches, more than 700 salting-houses and fish-oil factories were built in the archipelago. At this time, the street lamps of Paris burned fish oil from Bohuslän. Around 1810, however, the herring disappeared causing serious economic consequences.

THE OLD TOWN HALL IN LIDKÖPING

During the years of great catches, Swedes learned to eat herring from Bohuslän. Jonas Alströmer introduced the potato to Alingsås in the 1720s, and salt herring with potatoes eventually became a Swedish national dish. It was served with schnapps, which was easy to obtain. Excessive drinking was generally widespread until the emergence of the temperance movement in the mid-1800s.

During this time, a new age of religious fervor and sobriety was taking hold in western Sweden. A revival movement founded by pastor Henric Schartau was especially strong in Bohuslän.

During the first half of the nineteenth century, the woodland districts of Västra Götaland were finally penetrated by new communications. This was especially true of Tiveden, which for hundreds of years had been a natural barrier and frightening wilderness. The building of the Göta Canal and the expansion of the railways were the big breakthroughs.

The summer of 1868 has been called the summer without mercy. Crops failed to such a degree that the agricultural society in Skaraborg County published recipes for making bread with roots and bark. That catastrophic harvest was the main reason behind the great emigration to America.

In Västra Götaland, Dalsland suffered most from hunger and emigration.

Connections with foreign countries grew rapidly during the late 1800s and early 1900s. Västra Götaland was more and more a part of a larger unity, which was not just Sweden, but the entire European continent.

Not quite two years after Gothenburg's founder, Gust II Adolph, fell at the battle of Lützen, the estates of the realm – that is, Parliament – adopted a constitution which divided Sweden into governorships. These served as the basis for our present-day system of counties.

On January 1, 1998, reforms in the old county system led to the birth of the new County of Västra Götaland. This new county embraces both the ancient territories of the Goths and the former Norwegian province of Ranrike, which is now Bohuslän.

Indeed, the County of Västra Götaland has hundreds of years of history behind it.

Göran Behre

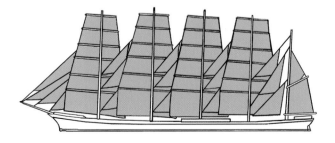

APPETIZER

Anchovy-potato salad

This salad is especially good on potato bread.
If it is unavailable, serve with whole-grain bread.
Try to make mustard sauce from scratch; it's so
much better than commercially prepared.
Restaurateur Bengt Petersen has offered his recipe.

PREPARATION TIME: *20 minutes*
plus 10 minutes for sauce

FOUR SERVINGS
1 onion
vegetable oil
1 hard-cooked egg
8 cold, boiled new potatoes
6 Swedish-style anchovy fillets
2 tablespoons anchovy brine
1 tablespoon each, parsley, chives, dill
2 dl (3/4 cup) crème fraiche or dairy sour cream

Mustard sauce:
2 tablespoons sugar
1 tablespoon vinegar
6 tablespoons sweet-strong Swedish mustard
2 tablespoons oil
2 tablespoons chopped fresh dill

Mince onion and sauté in a little oil until soft.
Chop egg, dice potatoes, chop anchovies.
Combine all ingredients except crème fraiche
carefully with a spoon.
Fold crème fraiche into anchovy mixture.
Serve on potato bread or whole grain bread.

SAUCE:
Dissolve sugar in vinegar and add mustard.
Whisk in oil in a thin stream and fold in dill.

TO SERVE:
Garnish with chive blossoms and serve with
mustard sauce.

BEVERAGE SUGGESTION: This is one of the most
Swedish of sandwich fillers. A light beer, perhaps
with a glass of schnapps, preferably flavored with
caraway, is the perfect accompaniment.

Ulrik Lindelöv, Alingsås

APPETIZER

Vegetable packet

This vegetarian starter features Swedish root vegetables and Asian wrappers. For a more traditional
packet, use puff pastry.

PREPARATION TIME: *20 minutes*
DEEP-FRYING TEMPERATURE: *170-80°C (350°F)*
SERVING SUGGESTION: *Serve with crème fraiche.*

FOUR SERVINGS
1 onion
2 carrots
2 parsnips
200 g (7 oz) celeriac
butter
salt and pepper
1 dl (scant 1/2 cup) crème fraiche or dairy sour cream
4 spring roll sheets
vegetable oil

Shred vegetables. Sauté in butter. Season with salt
and pepper. Transfer to a bowl and stir in crème
fraiche. Cool to lukewarm.
Divide filling among egg roll wrappers. Fold over
sides, then roll up. Moisten edge of dough to seal.
Deep-fry just before serving.

Café Mikaelsgården, Vårgårda

APPETIZER

Anchovy-gratinéed mussels

Mussels can be prepared in many ways. This dish is rich in flavor, with piquancy provided by both garlic and anchovies.

PREPARATION TIME: *20 minutes*
OVEN TEMPERATURE: *250°C (475°F)*

FOUR SERVINGS
1 onion
4 garlic cloves
4 dl (1 2/3 cups) white wine
1 kg (2 1/4 lb) mussels
5 anchovies
olive oil
5 dl (2 cups) whipping cream
1 tablespoon instant blending flour
chopped parsley

Chop onion, mince garlic. Place half the onion and all the garlic in a large saucepan with wine and mussels. Cover and cook unto mussels open, about 5 minutes. Discard any which do not open. Remove mussels and keep warm. Strain cooking liquid.
Chop anchovies. Sauté with remaining onion in olive oil. Add cooking liquid and cream.
Simmer several minutes. Thicken with flour. The sauce should not be too thick.
Preheat grill. Remove mussels from shells and divide among four individual ovenproof dishes. Season sauce to taste. Pour over mussels and grill until bubbly. Sprinkle with chopped parsley and serve.

Robert Widman, Nösunds Värdshus

MAIN DISH

Sole/flounder with orange-green pepper sauce

Sole is considered the most sophisticated of fish, and it has a lovely flavor and texture. This dish features interesting, exciting flavors.

PREPARATION TIME: *50 minutes,*
including 30 minutes marinating time

FOUR SERVINGS
600 g (1 1/3 lb) fillets of sole or flounder
grated rind of 2 oranges
50 g (3 tablespoons) butter
3 dl (1 1/4cups) fish stock
5 dl (2 cups) Noilly Prat
(dry vermouth)
2 dl (3/4 cup) white wine
1 dl (1/2 cup) whipping cream
2 tablespoons green pepper berries
salt and pepper
1 tablespoon chopped mint

Halve fillets along central line. Make a diagonal slit in the thickest part of the fillet and pull the thin tail section through the hole. Sprinkle with half the orange rind and marinate about 30 minutes. Heat half the butter in a sauté pan. Lightly sauté fillets. Add stock, vermouth and wine.
Poach 3-5 minutes. Remove fillets and keep warm. Add cream and pepper berries and reduce over high heat until half the original amount remains. Whisk in remaining butter. Season with salt and pepper.
Pour sauce over fillets and garnish with orange rind and mint leaves.

Robert Widman, Nösunds Värdshus

MAIN DISH

Salt-baked wild goose breast

Geese taste much better than they sound. Young geese are delicacies, but older geese defy both fire and water, according to Dr. Hagdahl.

PREPARATION TIME: *About 90 minutes*
OVEN TEMPERATURE: *225°C (425°F)*

FOUR SERVINGS
1 wild goose, about 2-2 1/2 kg (4 1/4 - 5 lb)

Stock:
Carcass and legs of goose
2 carrots
2 parsnips
150 g (5 oz) celeriac
1 onion
about 2 liters (8 cups) water
1 bay leaf
5 black peppercorns

Salt crust:
4 dl (1 1/2 cups) salt
2 dl (3/4 cup) flour
water

Sauce:
1 dl (scant 1/2 cup) sugar
3 dl (1 1/4 cups) red wine
3 dl (1 1/4 cups) duck stock
salt and pepper
2 teaspoons cornstarch
stirred into 1 tablespoon
cold water

16 almond potatoes
2 carrots
1 parsnip
4 shallots
butter

Carve out breasts and remove legs of the goose. Use legs for stock, as they are almost impossible to get tender. Set aside breasts.
Clean and cut stock vegetables into small chunks. Sauté with carcass and legs to a rich brown. Transfer to a large pot, add seasonings and water to cover. Simmer until vegetables are soft. Strain stock and reduce until rich and brown but not bitter.
Make a soft dough of salt and flour, adding water a little bit at a time.
Cover goose breasts with dough. Place in an oven-proof dish and bake until they reach an internal temperature of 73°C (132°F), about one hour. Wrap in foil and let rest at least 10 minutes before serving.
Melt sugar in a skillet and add wine. Reduce until syrupy. Add stock and reduce somewhat. Season to taste and thicken with cornstarch mixture.
Clean, peel and cut potatoes, carrots and parsnip into batons. Parboil a few minutes in lightly salted water. Peel shallots and cut into wedges. Brown in butter.

TO SERVE:
Open salt crust and remove goose breasts. Slice. Divide vegetables among four deep plates, then add sauce. Top with slices of goose breast. Add a little more sauce.

Gunnar Malm, Restaurant Gabriel, Gothenburg

MAIN DISH

Moose burgers
with rosemary potatoes

These really taste of the forest! The wild mushrooms add a lot of flavor. Ground game is an interesting alternative to ground beef and pork.

PREPARATION TIME: *About 1 hour*
OVEN TEMPERATURE: *200°F (400°C)*
SERVING SUGGESTION: *Serve with grilled tomatoes and steamed broccoli.*

FOUR SERVINGS
Rosemary potatoes:
6 medium potatoes
2 tablespoons vegetable oil
1 teaspoon salt
1 tablespoon dried rosemary

Burgers:
500 g (1 1/4 lb) ground moose, deer or other game
1 egg
50 g (2 oz) red bell pepper
1 dl (1/2 cup) blanched wild mushrooms (can use canned)
1 1/2 teaspoons salt
1/4 teaspoon pepper
butter

Sauce:
3 dl (1 1/4 cups) pan juices
2 teaspoons flour stirred into 1 tablespoon water
6 crushed juniper berries
salt and pepper

Scrub potatoes well and halve lengthwise. Brush with oil, then sprinkle with salt and rosemary. Bake about 20 minutes.
Combine ground meat and egg. Mince pepper and add with mushrooms and seasonings. Make eight burgers and fry 4 minutes per side. Transfer burgers to a serving platter and keep warm.

SAUCE:
Deglaze frying pan with 3 dl (1 1/4 cups) water. Whisk in flour mixture. Add juniper berries and salt and pepper to taste. Simmer at least three minutes.

Lena Ryberg, Sandra Loft Svensson, Mariestad

MAIN DISH

Chanterelle pie

Years ago, mushrooms were eaten only by the wealthy. Common folk did not feel mushrooms were worth anything other than something to sell to city folk or to feed their cattle.

PREPARATION TIME: *About 50 minuter*
OVEN TEMPERATURE: *200°C (400°F) for pie shell; 175°C (350°F) for filling*
SERVING SUGGESTION: *Serve with a green salad.*

FOUR SERVINGS
Pie crust:
3 dl (1 1/4 cups) flour
130 g (4 3/4 oz) butter
2 tablespoons cold water

Filling:
250 g (9 oz) fresh chanterelles (or 200 g (7 oz) canned)
1 garlic clove
1 tomato
1/2 yellow bell pepper
1/2 dl (3 1/2 tablespoons) chopped leek
2 dl (1 cup) grated Swiss cheese

Custard:
4 eggs
4 dl (1 2/3 cups) full fat milk
1 teaspoon salt
1 teaspoon white pepper
1 teaspoon vegetable bouillon granules

Place pie crust ingredients in a food processor. Process until dough begins to pull away from the sides. Form a ball, flatten and cover with plastic wrap. Refrigerate about 15 minutes.
Press pastry into an ovenproof dish or quiche pan and bake on center oven shelf about 10 minutes, until golden.
Clean mushrooms and cut into bitesize pieces. Mince garlic. Sauté without added fat until all liquid has evaporated.
Slice tomato and shred pepper. Arrange mushrooms and vegetables in pre-baked crust.
Top with cheese.
Whisk egg, milk and seasonings. Pour over filling. Bake about 20 minutes, until custard has set and turned golden.

Lisette Klingström and Erika Magnusson, Skövde

DESSERT

Månsagårn's apple pancake

This apple pancake has a lovely crispy exterior. It is quite a substantial dessert, which is perfect after a soup or other light main dish.

PREPARATION TIME: *45 minutes*
OVEN TEMPERATURE: *200°C (400°F)*

FOUR – SIX SERVINGS
Pancake batter:
2 eggs
4 dl (1 2/3 cups) flour
5 dl (2 cups) milk
1 tablespoon sugar

Filling:
6-8 apples
2 teaspoons cinnamon
1 1/2 dl (2/3 cup)
chopped hazelnuts
1/2 dl (3 1/2 tablespoons) sunflower seeds
1 dl (1/3 cup) pearl sugar or crushed sugar cubes

Place pancake batter ingredients in a blender and blend until smooth. Pour into an ovenproof dish or small oven tray.
Peel and core apples. Cut into quarters.
Arrange on batter and sprinkle with cinnamon, nuts, seeds and sugar.
Bake about 30 minutes.

Ann-Cathrine Carlsson, Vara

DESSERT

Bohuslän egg cheese

There are many types of egg cheese. In this recipe, vinegar concentrate is used as a curdling agent. It is probably an old recipe and alludes to how it was served as well. It was eaten with savory foods more often than as a dessert with fruit preserves.

PREPARATION TIME: : *One hour plus 3-4 hours for draining and 30 minutes for tempering before serving*
SERVING SUGGESTION: *Serve with smoked ham, meatballs and bread.*

FOUR SERVINGS
3 liters (quarts) full fat milk
6 eggs
4 teaspoons vinegar concentrate
1/2 dl (3 1/2 tablespoons) sugar

Pour milk into a heavy saucepan.
Beat eggs until smooth and add vinegar concentrate.
Add egg mixture to milk.
Cook over medium heat, stirring constantly with a wooden spoon, to make sure mixture does not burn. Do not allow to boil.
When mixture gets hot enough, it separates.
Add a little cold water if it separates unevenly.
Once separation process has begun, it does not take more than a few minutes. If it takes too long, egg cheese will be hard.
The mixture should separate evenly all over.
Remove pan from heat and let rest 5-10 minutes.
Remove egg cheese with a slotted spoon and place in an egg cheese mold, layering with sugar to taste.
Let whey drain off. Refrigerate.
Remove egg cheese from refrigerator about 30 minutes before serving.
Unmold onto a flat serving dish with a rim.

Astrid Svensson, Kode

DESSERT

Harvest torte with lemon mousse

This lovely torte decorated with black currants is served at Cesarstugan in Östra Tunhem.
The recipe has been adapted for the home kitchen. Bavarian cream is used instead of mousse, because it is more stable. The jelly is made with elderberry juice, which goes well with lemon and currant.

PREPARATION TIME: *50 minutes plus one hour in the refrigerator*
SERVING SUGGESTION: *190°C (375°F)*

TWELVE SERVINGS
Sponge layers:
3 eggs
3 dl (1 1/4 cups) sugar
1 dl (scant 1/2 cup) hot water
3 dl (1 1/4 cups) flour
1 1/2 teaspoons baking powder

Lemon bavarian:
2 1/2 teaspoons powdered gelatin
2 1/2 tablespoons water
2 eggs
3/4 dl (1/3 cup) sugar
grated rind and juice of 1 lemon
2 dl (3/4 cup) whipping cream

Jelly:
6 gelatin sheets
5 dl (2 cups) elderberry juice

Garnish:
3 dl (1 1/4 cups) black currants
whipped cream
yellow marzipan roses
green marzipan leaves

SPONGE LAYERS:
Grease and flour a 22 cm (9") springform pan.
Beat eggs and sugar until light and lemon-colored.
Add water, a little at a time. Combine dry ingredients and add, mixing well.
Pour into prepared pan and bake on lowest oven shelf about 35 minutes.
Cool before removing from pan.

LEMON BAVARIAN:
Sprinkle powdered gelatin over water to soften, about 5 minutes. Melt over low heat.
Separate eggs. Beat egg yolks and sugar until light and lemon colored. Add lemon rind and juice and melted gelatin.
Whip cream and fold into egg yolk mixture.
Beat egg white until stiff and fold into egg yolk mixture.
The mixture should be light and fluffy.
Refrigerate until half-set, about one hour.

JELLY:
Soak gelatin sheets in cold water to soften, about 5 minutes. Heat juice. Squeeze gelatin sheets to remove excess water and add to juice.
Stir until dissolved. Refrigerate until somewhat thickened.

TO ASSEMBLE:
Divide sponge base into three layers.
Spread each with lemon bavarian. Stack.
Clean and dry currants and arrange over top layer of bavarian cream. Cover with jelly.
When set, decorate with whipped cream, marzipan roses and leaves.

Idea from Cesarstugan, Östra Tunhem

Whole grain rolls

These chewy rolls give the jaws good exercise.

PREPARATION TIME: *About 70 minutes plus soaking overnight*
OVEN TEMPERATURE: *250°C (475°F)*

40 TEA CAKES
1 liter (4 cups) boiling water
2 dl (3/4 cup) cracked rye
2 dl (3/4 cup) cracked wheat
8 dl (3 1/3 cups) coarse rye flour
5 dl (2 cups) milk
1/2 dl (3 1/2 tablespoons) vegetable oil
100 g (3 1/2 oz) fresh yeast
1 tablespoon light corn syrup
4 teaspoons salt
about 2 liters (8 cups) flour

OLD ADAGE
Bought bread is a waste of taste

Combine water, cracked rye, cracked wheat and rye flour. Let soak overnight.
The next day, heat milk to 37°C (98°F). Combine with oil, yeast, syrup and salt, mixing well. Add rye dough. Knead in flour, then knead 5 minutes in a mixer with a dough hook or 10 minutes by hand.
Cover and let rise 30 minutes.
Divide dough into four parts.
Roll out each piece of dough. Using a 10 cm (4") cutter, cut 10 rounds from each.
Cover and let rise 30 minutes.
Bake on center oven shelf about 8 minutes.
Stack and cover to cool.

Vänga mill, a few miles from Fristad

Garlic-basil bread

This bread, with its trendy flavors, is especially good with soup and salad.

PREPARATION TIME: *About 90 minutes*
OVEN TEMPERATURE: *225°C (425°F)*

2 MONKEY BREADS
50 g (1 1/3 oz) fresh yeast
5 dl (2 cups) water
250 g (9 oz) low-fat cottage cheese
1 tablespoon vegetable oil
2 teaspoons salt
2 tablespoons light corn syrup
2 minced garlic cloves
2 tablespoons dried basil or 1/2 dl (3 1/2 tablespoons) fresh chopped basil
2 dl (3/4 cup) whole wheat flour
1 – 1 1/3 liters (4 – 5 1/2 cups) flour
1 egg
3 tablespoons poppy seeds or sesame seeds

OLD ADAGE
Hit the dough too hard and our husband may hit you

Crumble yeast in a large mixer bowl. Heat water to 37°C (98°F) and pour over yeast. Stir until dissolved. Add cheese, oil, salt, syrup, garlic, basil and almost all the flour. Knead 5 minutes in a mixer with a dough hook or 10 minutes by hand.
Cover and let rise 30 minutes.
Turn dough out onto a floured board and knead until smooth and elastic. Form into small balls. Pack tightly together to form two round breads. Place on cookie sheets lined with baking parchment. Cover and let rise 30 minutes.
Brush with beaten egg and sprinkle with seeds.
Bake about 25 minutes, until golden. Cool on a rack.

Christina Asplund, Gothenburg

Recipes in alphabetical order

Cuisine from Sweden's West at its Best

Contents see page 4

ADDITIONAL PHOTOS
Bildbyrån i Göteborg AB
Anders Hesslegård
Johnér Bildbyrå
Naturfotografernas Bildbyrå AB
Falköpings Turistbyrå
Margareta Boman
Louise Thordin
Per Landén
Astrid Bergman Sucksdorff; pages 48, 67, 68, 69, 70, 71, 195

❧

ADDITIONAL ILLUSTRATIONS
Georges Didier; pages 14, 170, 189
Pontus Berglund

❧

THANKS TO
Rörstrand
Kinnasand
Tomas Bengtsson, Falbygdens Ost
Hummerakademien, Hunnebostrand
Lenas Växter, Hällum, Vara
Qlaz Eliason, Hilda Nilssons Ost, Stora Saluhallen, Göteborg
Bohusläns museum
Pååls Bröd AB
Gunnebo Slott
Katja Palmblad
Karin Wagner
Marika Sandahl
Nordfalks